DATE DUE			
FEB 2 9 1988			
MAR 2 8 2007			
MAY 3 1 2007			

NATURALISM

NATURALISM

BY

JAMES BISSETT PRATT

KENNIKAT PRESS
Port Washington, N. Y./London

NATURALISM

Copyright © 1939 by Yale University Press
Renewed 1967 by Mrs. Catherine Pratt
Reprinted 1973 by Kennikat Press in an unaltered
and unabridged edition with permission
Library of Congress Catalog Card No.: 72-85424
ISBN 0-8046-1729-5

Manufactured by Taylor Publishing Company   Dallas, Texas

THE
MAHLON POWELL FOUNDATION

MAHLON POWELL—1842–1928
WABASH, INDIANA

*Extract from the last Will and Testament of
Mahlon Powell:*

Having entertained a desire for many years
to assist in the cause of a higher education for
the young men and women of our state and na-
tion, and to that end provide a fund to be held in
trust for the same, and to select a proper school
or university where the same would continue in
perpetuity, I will, devise and bequeath all of the
real and personal property that I possess and
of which I die seized to the Trustees of Indiana
University, Bloomington, Indiana, to be held by
them and their successors in office forever, the
Income only to be used and applied in the support and maintenance of a *Chair* in *Philosophy*
in said institution, and to be dedicated and forever known as "The Mahlon Powell Professor-
ship in Philosophy" of said University.

*In accordance with the provisions of this be-
quest, the Trustees of Indiana University have
established a Chair in Philosophy on The Mahlon Powell Foundation. Each year a Visiting
Professor will be invited to fill this Chair. The
third lecturer on The Mahlon Powell Foundation
is Professor James Bissett Pratt of Williams
College.*

WILLIAM LOWE BRYAN

CONTENTS

Preface   ix

I. What "Naturalism" Means and
   How It Began   1

II. Naturalism, Life, and Evolution   47

III. Naturalism and Mind   95

IV. Naturalism, Morality, and Re-
    ligion   143

Index   179

PREFACE

I COULD write a pretty good critical review of this book. It would not be difficult to show that the organic and teleological ways of looking at life, evolution, and the world in general, herein suggested, as well as some of my proposals concerning the possible relations between Naturalism and Religion, are far from demonstrable. Criticism of this sort might be sprightly; but I am not sure it would be entirely fair. For in so far as Naturalism is taken as a systematic description or theory of the world, it is frankly speculative; and taken in this sense it has several forms, none of them demonstrable. For the type of naturalistic theory I have suggested I have claimed nothing more than probability, nothing more than is proposed in any philosophical speculation of an empirical sort. As I view it, the problem proposed to every philosopher might be worded thus: Given these and these facts, what hypothesis best unifies them and best illuminates the world we live in?

Of course the principal point I have tried to make is the distinction between a crude and a critical Naturalism; and the importance of identifying Naturalism not with any particular theory but with its empirical method and its truth-seeking aim. My little book I consider a defense of Naturalism against its most dangerous enemies; the majority of whom are usually found in the ranks of the "naturalists."

JAMES BISSETT PRATT

Williamstown, Mass., March 17, 1939.

NATURALISM

CHAPTER I

WHAT "NATURALISM" MEANS
AND HOW IT BEGAN

IT is not, I trust, too much to hope that,
however dull these lectures may turn out
to be, the *subject* of them at any rate will
have an immediate appeal to most of those
who are so courageous—or so ill advised—as
to come and hear them. For the open-minded
and persistent study of Nature—which,
roughly speaking, is what I take Naturalism
to be—has been very central to man's thought
and to his practical progress ever since man
began to think at all: and beginning with the
Renaissance, and particularly in very recent
years, European philosophy has become more
and more "naturalistic." It should, therefore, be worth at least a few hours of our
time to take stock of our situation, to make
a brief review of what Naturalism has been
and has done in the past, and at least to guess
in what direction it is facing as it fronts the
future.

If we are going to discuss Naturalism to
any purpose, however, plainly we must first

of all make up our minds what we are going to mean by the term. It is, as I have suggested, the study of Nature; but the term needs to be made much more specific than this. And, to begin with, Naturalism will not be worth discussing if we define it in a way that will make it, from the start, indefensible. Thus, if we make the term synonymous with some dogmatic form of extreme Materialism or Mechanism we may as well spare ourselves the tedium of lecturing or listening to lectures upon it. To make such an identification, moreover, would be exceedingly unfair to the leaders and the rank and file of the great naturalistic movement. For your genuine upholder of Naturalism honestly wants to know the truth. Investigation of the real world, not propaganda of some favorite dogma, is his chief interest. Too often in religious and idealistic circles is Naturalism spoken of as a kind of evil conspiracy against all that is spiritual and ideal, a devil's invention with only malevolent aims. Such a picture is sheer caricature. There are, indeed, in every generation, a few loud-mouthed, second-rate naturalistic talkers, of sadistic tendencies, who delight in undermining and ridiculing all that their neighbors find sacred. Your true naturalistic philosopher—for the sake of brevity let me hereafter speak of him as a "naturalist" without confusing him in your minds with the biologist—your genuine naturalist has little or nothing in common with the bombastic atheist and materialist of an outgrown age. To the careless and inattentive he may, indeed, seem to resemble the noisy and vulgar iconoclast, because he is brave enough to face and to accept unpleasant and even appalling facts, provided they be facts. But the motive that prompts this is not love of destruction but love of truth. An earnest and courageous desire to find out and face the truth, no matter what it may be, is, indeed, the first characteristic of your genuine upholder of Naturalism.

In our effort to understand what Naturalism is it may be helpful for us to begin by noting some of the things which Naturalism is not and some of the things which it opposes. And, first of all, it is in sharp and conscious contrast to the Will-to-Believe. Its aim, as we have seen, is not propaganda; neither is it self-deception. It is seeking not a pleasant feeling state nor a comfortable belief, but the truth. And Naturalism believes that the truth is what it is, no matter what we think about it. Nature, the world of reality, has a character, a structure of its

own, and our opinions are true only in so far
as they conform to this actual situation.
There is much in common between Naturalism and the school of thought known as
Instrumentalism: but in so far as Instrumentalism denies to Reality an antecedent
structure of its own, Naturalism will be unable to join forces with it. The world which
Naturalism wishes to study is not determined
nor given its character by our belief, nor by
our will to believe.

Another form of the Will-to-Believe which
the naturalist cannot share is the attitude of
the man who, more or less deliberately, allows
his view of Reality to be colored or determined by the romantic and poetic tendencies
of the human mind. This does not mean that
the naturalistic view will necessarily be un-
poetic or ugly. That will be as it will be.
But the influences which, in the last analysis,
determine the naturalistic *Weltanschauung*
are not the appeal of the beautiful or the
pathetic, the tragic or the pleasing, but unprejudiced reason and empirical observation.
The naturalist may or may not be a poet:
but while he is investigating the nature of
Reality he is bound to be a realist. He may
be fond of poetry and he will be fond of
knowledge; but he takes each of the two

"straight," as the drinkers say. Mixing drinks of this sort is something he does not believe in. He cannot agree that "beauty is truth, truth beauty"; in fact he is so prosaic as to question whether Keats' line really means anything at all.

You see, the gentleman with whom we have to deal throughout these four lectures is a pretty dull fellow, perhaps not very interesting. If we are going to like him it must be for some solid qualities of straightforward honesty and loyalty to the truth—even should the truth turn out to be colorless or distressing. He is bound to offend many of the aesthetically and romantically minded. And I fear he is bound also to offend many of the religiously minded. For, I suppose, the point of view with which Naturalism is most obviously to be contrasted is Supernaturalism. The contrast in the first place is chiefly verbal, for "Supernaturalism" is a vague and ambiguous term, needing definition quite as badly as does "Naturalism." But there can be no doubt that, even aside from obviously hostile names, there is a real clash between the two points of view. Some analysis of Supernaturalism is needed if the real opposition is to be brought to light.

The term clearly presupposes some con-

cept of "Nature," and the concept of Nature
is a product of the naturalistic point of view.
Probably I should not have used the word
"product," but a better one for the purpose
I cannot find. That search for the truth about
the world we live in and depend upon, that
inborn tendency toward science which characterizes the naturalistic movement, does not
so much produce the concept of Nature as
take it for granted. It does so because without it success in both man's practical and his
theoretical aims would be out of the question.
Primitive man found himself in the presence
of powers much greater than his own, and he
had to control, or at least avoid, them on pain
of utter destruction. But in order to avoid
the enemies with which organic and inorganic
Nature is replete, and also to utilize the
natural forces which to some extent could
be controlled and directed, two things were
necessary. He must have the coöperation of
his fellows, and he and they must know what
to expect from Nature. Hence the necessity
of communication between men in dealing
with general situations, the necessity of con-
ceiving these in universal and descriptive
terms, and of linking these conceived situations and events in repeatable series in such
fashion that the appearance of one member

will be a sign of the coming of the next. Thus, in an unexpressed and purely implicit, but still very real fashion, a concept of an orderly system of Nature began to be built up in men's minds by the very practical necessities of life itself.

But it was not only the pragmatic need of dealing efficiently with the environment that led man to investigate the nature of the world in which he lived, and to think of it in terms of an orderly system. Besides the pragmatic motive there was also a purely intellectual one. Even the animals, at least the higher ones, seem to possess what Professor Mc-Dougall calls the instinct of curiosity. In man this native desire, reinforced by the rise of reason and the urge to use it, has developed into a theoretical passion, so that, as Aristotle expressed it in that immortal first sentence of the *Metaphysics*, "All men by nature desire knowledge."

Both this theoretical urge and the practical need of dealing with confusing situations have led man, the thinker, to seek as large a degree of simplicity in his conclusions as is compatible with the empirically discovered facts. The simple conception is more easily and more effectively handled than the complex and multiform, and the dictum not to multiply hypotheses beyond necessity was implicit in the practical situation at the very beginning of applied science. Corresponding to this practical tendency toward simplicity is an intellectual tendency toward monistic views. For one of the principal aims of thinking is explanation and one of the chief types of explanation consists in placing individuals in groups, species within genera —in short, reducing the seeming many to some underlying One.

To come back now to Naturalism and Supernaturalism—various practical and theoretical influences inevitably led man to build up a common and public conception of the existent world which was steadily enlarged and modified by further experience and new insights, and handed on from generation to generation. Such a body of facts and theories, as we have seen, necessarily embodies order, regularity, the means of explanation and anticipation. Thus was built up something like a crude philosophic or scientific concept of Nature. When, now, some event occurred which did not fit into the accepted system, a choice between three different attitudes toward it was possible. One might totally ignore the new evidence and simply stick to the good old theory without modification. This has occasionally been the attitude of a crude, conservative, and dogmatic Naturalism. Secondly, one might strive to see whether by some ingenious interpretation of the new evidence, or some modification of the old system, the two might be reconciled, and thus a richer and also more critical Naturalism be attained. Or, thirdly, one might—especially if the new evidence pointed in a desired direction—give up the ideal of natural law and cosmic consistency and accept uncritically the new phenomenon without relating it to any orderly conception of Nature. This third attitude, which really makes the new datum an expression of disorder, was thoroughly distasteful to those most deeply interested in the progress of human knowledge, in the power of man to explain, to anticipate, and to understand. For to understand an event is to see it in its relations; and the isolated and non-ordered event has no relations save purely external and casual ones which it may shed on its next appearance. Those who, in the earliest times or in the present, have felt but a minimum of interest in the intellectual grasp of events, and in the progress and sureness of man's control over his environment, have constituted the raw material from which the school of the supernaturalists has been made.

There is a group of thinkers—or at least of believers—sometimes wrongly identified with the supernaturalists, to whom, for a different reason, all good naturalists find themselves quite as fundamentally opposed as they are to the schools of thought just dealt with. These are the believers from authority. Two quite different types of mind are sometimes classified under this heading. The first consists of very numerous individuals whose opinions are based upon habit and upon the lazy man's dislike of the effort of thought, or the timid man's fear of upsetting his comfort. These people, like the rest of us, receive in childhood certain beliefs from the generation that preceded them, and owing to the conservatism and inertia of human nature not only cling to these beliefs almost unchanged to the end of their days, but usually resent, and often violently resist, any new ideas out of harmony with the beliefs that were impressed upon their minds by their revered elders in the days of their infantile innocence. Quite different, upon the surface at any rate, are the other upholders of authority. These are willing and often eager to discuss with you the relative merits of old ideas and new, and ready to defend by arguments and logic the beliefs which they hold. The arguments are ultimately, of course, the reasoned defenses of the trustworthiness of the authority upon which their beliefs are based. How, they ask, can the puny thinking power of the little individual, born but yesterday, compare with the massive strength of tradition—tradition which is in fact the felted and condensed outcome of the race thinking? How repeatedly the individual is mistaken; but who can rationally doubt *quod ubique, quod semper, quod ab omnibus?* Is it not absurd to trust to the petty experiments and the very youthful guesses of a few so-called thinkers of this generation in preference to the obviously inspired insights of our ancient and inspired Scriptures, or the *ex cathedra* pronouncements of Holy Church?

Against these defenders of tradition, of both sorts, the naturalist is bound to take his stand. For him nothing is proved true by the fact that many people have believed it. And as for the authority of a Church or of some ancient and revered book, the trustworthiness of its statements, its truth-value—that is just one of the things that need investigation and which can be accepted only on the basis of

facts and of a logic that does not take for
granted at the beginning of the argument
the conclusion which it is intended to prove.
The opposition of Naturalism to belief based
on authority is one of its most decisive characteristics.

As was indicated at the beginning of the
preceding paragraph, the founding of belief
upon authority must not be identified with
Supernaturalism. Not all supernaturalists
are authoritarians; and a great many authoritarians are to be found among those who most
loudly attack, and most scornfully reject,
Supernaturalism. Among the believers in authority must be classed all, or nearly all, of
the dogmatists, and these are legion. Whoever seeks to stop the mouths of opponents,
and to settle disputes, by the citation of
famous names or by a reference to that which
scriptum est is a dogmatist and an authoritarian, whether the name and book be pious
or secular, whether the writing be in the
Holy Scriptures or in the latest philosophical treatise of some distinguished natural
scientist.

Another and quite different school of
thought with which it is instructive to contrast Naturalism is Rationalism. Not that
Rationalism and Naturalism are always hos-

tile; on some issues they stand side by side against a common foe. Both are opposed to allowing one's wishes to influence one's philosophic attitude; both are opposed to unreasoned trust in authority. They differ in interest and in method. Rationalism is interested chiefly in logic and the processes and outcome of pure *a priori* thought: Naturalism is interested in the physical, spatial, temporal, human world. Rationalism investigates the realm of essence, Naturalism the realm of existence. This, I confess, is so brief a characterization of the two schools as to merit serious criticism if taken too literally and too exclusively. It is intended only as a general statement, an indication of direction rather than a definition. As a result of this difference of interest, the two schools differ in methods employed. Naturalism, like Rationalism, of course makes use of reason, but it also trusts to and relies largely upon empirical evidence. It follows that the conception of the Real which it builds up is rich in detail, lacking in the unity and the perfection of form which rationalistic systems possess, and only partly sure of its results. It considers its conclusions probably true, but not absolutely necessary. The Real of Rationalism, on the other hand, is thoroughly monistic and at the same time so poor in detail as to be almost or entirely formal and lacking in empirical content. The rationalist wants everything explained till it is as luminous as the Laws of Thought. The empiricist, on the other hand, is willing to take things as they are, if they really are, and not ask why. When Sandin, the young aborigine of Borneo, reported in a recent *Atlantic*, reached Africa on his long journey, he was at first astonished at the temperature, and, to quote his words, said to men, " 'Why is it so cold in one place and so hot in another?' And one said, 'Well, because it is just that way.' So I said, 'Yes, probably that is just the way it is.' " Sandin, you see, was a good empiricist.

There are two sub-types of Rationalism and these sustain rather different relations to Naturalism. One kind of rationalist is simply not interested in the world of space, time, and human life, but only in the "eternal verities," the necessary truths; not in the realm of existence, but solely in the realm of essence. Between this type of rationalist and the naturalist there can hardly be any quarrel. They can no more collide than can two locomotives moving on different tracks. But there is a type of rationalist who is not content to confine himself to the realm of essence and who believes that pure reason without assistance from the brute facts of experience can be an adequate guide to all the genuinely philosophical problems of our real world. Between such a rationalist and your realistic naturalist there is bound to be trouble.

For there is often a close relation between this type of Rationalism and the Will-to-Believe, a relation not always recognized but very real. The rationalist who deals with this existent world at all is pretty sure to insist that within it there is no mere datum, but everything is thoroughly explicable and logically necessary: "the real is the rational and the rational the real." Now if we ask how the rationalist knows this to be the case, he cannot, of course, appeal in its defense to empirical evidence, for that would be to surrender his position. But neither can he prove in *a priori* fashion that it must be so: for there is nothing self-contradictory in the opposite view. His ultimate appeal is therefore of an essentially emotional or aesthetic sort. He is unwilling to consider the hypothesis that this good world should contain within it anything not necessitated by Reason. His position is not unlike that of the scholars and explorers during the century after Columbus who took it as a matter of course that there *must* be a northwest passage. As Prescott has put it, they "could not believe that Nature had worked on a plan so repugnant, apparently, to the interests of humanity as to interpose, through the whole length of the great continent, such a barrier to communication between the adjacent waters." *

What has been said of the rise of Naturalism and of the contrast it sustains to certain opposing systems enables us to come now to a closer determination of its nature. Naturalism as we have viewed it is characterized by three things: by its aim, by its method, and by its resulting system. All three are genuine parts of Naturalism. But the system it builds up is less important to it, less fundamental, less permanent than its method; and its method less permanent and essential than its aim. First of all, it wants the truth about the world we live in, whatever that may turn out to be. In order to attain this it makes use of the empirical method. And by the use of this method it builds up a picture of the universe. It is plain that one cannot define Naturalism by any given picture, by any given theory or system. For its fidelity to its method and its aim prevent its being wholly and finally com-

* *Conquest of Mexico,* III, 259.

mitted to any theory, and keep it perpetually adding to, subtracting from, and modifying whatever concept or system it may have built up. It is hardly conceivable that the time will ever come when it will reach an absolutely complete and final system, or cease changing at least in detail the best system it shall have constructed.

It may be objected that the concept of Naturalism I have suggested makes it practically identical with empirical philosophy. The criticism, if it be one, is well taken: but I should not consider it an objection to my position. Unless we are to define Naturalism to begin with in a fashion that will make it ultimately untenable, unless we are, in fact, to identify it with one or another of the schools of thought to which it is fundamentally opposed, we cannot find its central nature in any fixed metaphysics or system of ontological concepts. The conclusions, the pictures of the universe, which its adherents through the centuries have supported, differ notably in detail. The one characteristic common to all the naturalistic systems is the persistent attempt to find out, by all the resources of empirical fact and unprejudiced logic, the truth about the world we live in. A brief review of the early development and history of Naturalism will, I trust, make this even more clear.

It is not uncommon to trace the parentage of Naturalism to Leucippus and Democritus. Such a view places the rise of Naturalism far too late in the history of human thought. It began much farther back than any of the "Histories of Greek Philosophy" can go. It was prehistoric men that began it, the first thinkers who attempted to interpret the facts of experience in such a way as to throw some light on things and events as a whole. What was the first form of this naturalistic thought we do not know. Considerable evidence has been brought forward by anthropologists to indicate that the earliest interpretation of Nature was the *mana* theory. Tyler and Spencer thought it was Animism. Other hypotheses have been suggested. Whatever view we take upon this question, certainly the first attempts to interpret the facts of experience in a systematic way were exceedingly crude and the outcome exceedingly vague, and the rare desire to think clearly in terms of the evidence gave way again and again to the much commoner human urge to tell stories and spin out poetical and interesting myths. Poetry and naturalistic thought need not be rivals or foes, but especially in the

early years of the race and of the individual
they are likely to be. And in the Western
World, the first sharp and recorded advance
toward a pure Naturalism came about in the
sixth century B.C., when a few Greek thinkers,
some of whose names are known to us, "left
off telling tales," as Burnet has expressed it,*
and began the serious attempt to explain the
observed facts in impersonal terms.

The first name we find in this list, as everyone knows, is Thales. The important thing
about Thales was the question he propounded,
not the answer he suggested. What, he asked,
are all things made of? What is the one substance behind appearances? In the spirit of
this question there is much that is characteristic of Naturalism. Thales refused to be
satisfied with myths and stories and put his
wonder in terms which, not the imagination,
but reason and empirical investigation might
at least hope to resolve. His primal aim was
the actual truth, not the popularization of
some pet theory. This was the eternal value
of his quest. His method was in part that of
observation: though the observation was very
faulty. His final conclusion, or attempt at
system, was negligible. Dear old Father
Thales—in how many of his naturalistic

* *Early Greek Philosophy*, p. 8.

descendants have these family characteristics been repeated!

Of his several Greek followers perhaps the first to make a really fruitful suggestion in the building up of a naturalistic world scheme was Anaximenes. With his fellow Ionians he shared the common naturalistic desire for simplification, and he saw, as his predecessors had not seen, that if the seemingly diverse forms of matter were to be reduced to one type (as Thales and Anaximander had sought to do), some hypothesis must be proposed by which the one fundamental matter might be conceived as changing from one form to another. This hypothesis he found in the conception of rarefaction and condensation. Earth, water, air, fire, and whatsoever forms of matter there might be, differed from each other only in containing within them greater or smaller amounts of—or in being more or less tightly packed with—the fundamental and unchanging substance. This proposal was epoch-making, for it suggested a method by which quality might be translated into quantity, and measurable amounts of the same thing might be substituted for innumerable qualities, none of which were reducible to any other. This new conception was an invaluable tool

for advancing two of the persistent ambitions
of Naturalism—the theoretical demand for
increasing simplicity, and the pragmatic desire to view things in a way that should make
them easy for the practical, measuring intel-
lect to handle. The final outcome in Greek
philosophy of this crucial suggestion of
Anaximenes was the atomic theory of Leucippus and Democritus.

Naturalism is only one form of philosophy,
and by no means all the Greek philosophers
contributed to its development. The great
Parmenides, for whom Socrates is depicted
by Plato as having such reverence, was far
too fond of the *a priori* and had far too little
respect for the reports of experience to be
classed in the school we are studying.
Socrates himself and his great disciple Plato,
though as eager for the truth as any empiricist, centered their attention on problems that
lay out of the direct line of naturalistic
thought. Plato, in fact, appears to have considered the Ionian physical philosophy un-
worthy of serious consideration. Nor are the
Eleatics and Platonists the only members of
the great philosophic tradition of Greece who
are not to be numbered in the naturalistic
school. In that cradle of Western philosophy,
and in other Mediterranean lands, there were,

during the classical and the Hellenistic and
Roman periods of antiquity, many brilliant
minds who mixed with their desire to know
the truth so much preconception as to what
the truth must be, so much poetry, so much
"rationalism," so much of the Will-to-Believe, that the sum total of their influence was
rather to delay than to advance the progress
of Naturalism. No one can be classed in that
prosaic school who would rather be wrong
with Plato than right with his opponents.

But the Greek thinker who stood second
only to Plato certainly should be enumerated
among the naturalists. Aristotle is not, indeed, to be classified with Anaximenes and
Democritus among those students of Nature
who attempt to reduce all Reality to the
quantitatively measurable. He was very far
indeed from agreeing with the conclusions,
the system, of the atomists. But the primary
naturalistic aim—to find out the truth about
Nature—and the naturalistic, empirical, and
rational method were his in abundant measure. It seems, in fact, to have been his larger
loyalty to the principles of Empiricism that
led him to reject the conclusions of many of
his naturalistic predecessors. They were, in
his opinion, not empirical enough. Their
Atomism was to be criticized not because it

was Naturalism but because it was an incomplete and inadequate Naturalism. It neglected some of the most important facts of experience, or tried to explain them away by obviously inadequate guesses of an *a priori* sort. The atomistic hypothesis of Democritus is, in Aristotle's opinion, far too *thin* to account for the facts that we find. There is more to Nature than matter. Things have characters; they participate, as Plato said, in universals: change, motion, energy, growth, regular development, laws, life, mind—these are not to be explained by any mere congeries of atoms of the simple sort conceived by Leucippus and Democritus.

When these men and the principles of their kind had had their day [Aristotle writes], as the latter were found inadequate to generate the nature of things, men were forced by the truth itself to seek for some other kind of cause [than the purely material]. For surely it is not likely that either fire or earth or any such element should be the reason why things manifest goodness and beauty both in their being and in their coming to be: nor again could it be right to ascribe so great a matter to spontaneity and luck. When one man said, then, that reason was present—as in animals, so throughout nature—as the cause of the world and of all its order, he seemed like a sober man in contrast with the random talk of his predecessors.*

One may well refuse to accept Aristotle's naturalistic system, just as he refused to accept that of Democritus; but there can be little question that Aristotle's was far the more empirical of the two, and that the Atomism of his predecessors was, in comparison with his hypothesis, a thin and exceedingly inadequate representation of the reality with which experience presents us. More specifically, Aristotle enriched Naturalism by introducing into it the use of universals, by adding the concept of efficient causation, and by recognizing the seemingly teleological facts of life and mind and the need of giving them some adequate explanation. No system which leaves these out can vindicate itself as a true account of Nature or the Real.

This question of the place of the seemingly teleological in the Cosmos will face us again, but something should here be said as to the appropriate attitude to be taken toward it by the consistent naturalist. There are two motives which have led philosophers to the recognition of purpose within Nature, one

* *Metaphysics,* 984^b.

idealist, one empirical. Plato was dominated
by the former: the urge, namely, to explain
the facts of the world, combined with the conviction that the only type of explanation
consists in pointing out some good end which
the facts in question will tend to achieve. Thus
the Platonic Socrates in the *Phaedo* tells his
disciples of his delight in finding, some years
before, a book by Anaxagoras, and adds:

I rejoiced to think that I had found in
Anaxagoras a teacher of the causes of existence
such as I desired, and I imagined that he would
tell me first whether the earth is flat or round;
and then he would further explain the cause and
the necessity of this, and would teach me the
nature of the best and show that this was best;
and if he said that the earth was in the center,
he would explain that this position was the
best, and I should be satisfied if this were shown
to me, and not want any other sort of cause.
And I thought that I would then go on and ask
him about the sun and moon and stars, and that
he would explain to me their comparative swift-
ness, and their returnings and various states and
how their several affections, active and passive,
were all for the best. For I could not imagine
that when he spoke of mind as the disposer of
them, he would give any other account of their
being as they are, except that this was best;
and I thought that when he had explained to me

in detail the cause of each and the cause of all, he would go on to explain to me what was best for each and what was best for all.*

This type of insistence on teleology may have much to say for itself, but it is not Naturalism. It believes that purpose dominates the world, because it is convinced that explanation through purpose is the only thoroughly rational explanation. The upholders of this view can put up a strong case. It is interesting to recall that even so thorough-going an empiricist as William James can say:

If one talks of rationality and of reasons for things, and insists that they can't just come in spots, what *kind* of a reason can there ultimately be why anything should come at all? Talk of logic and necessity and categories and the absolute and the contents of the whole philosophical machine-shop as you will, the only *real* reason I can think of why anything should ever come is that *some one wishes it to be here.* It is *demanded,*—demanded, it may be, to give relief to no matter how small a fraction of the world's mass. This is *living reason,* and compared with it material causes and logical necessities are spectral things.†

* *Phaedo,* pp. 97–98.
† *Pragmatism,* pp. 288–289.

But it is to be noted that whether an empiricist agrees or does not agree that the only sort of rational explanation is teleological, he cannot, with Plato, draw from this the conclusion that therefore, necessarily, Reality *must be* ultimately dominated by Purpose. For in drawing such a conclusion he would be making use of a hidden major premise to the effect that Reality must be rationally explicable: must, that is, be ultimately rational and totally understandable. Plato and the Platonist may be willing and eager to say this quite explicitly; but no empiricist, and therefore no naturalist, will be able to make out and sign in advance any such blank check. *Is* the world ultimately rational in the sense implied? *Is* it totally understandable? Is the real the rational and the rational the real? These are questions the answers to which the naturalist will not seek to evolve out of his inner consciousness, nor to determine by some form of unquestionable intuition or the Will-to-Believe. Instead, he will go, in much humbler and quite prosaic fashion, to such facts as he can observe or collect, and thus try to find out whether the world appears to be wholly teleological, wholly bereft of purpose, or purposeful in some partial degree. Aristotle was in his youth an enthusiastic

Platonist, and to his dying day he never completely threw off the influence of his great teacher. His belief in a teleological aspect or element in the Cosmos was, especially in his earlier writings, to some extent of the Platonic sort. But the motive chiefly responsible for his conclusion that not only material and efficient causes but also final causes must be appealed to by the student of Nature was of a different type: a motive that has been profoundly influential in molding the conclusions of many naturalistic thinkers from his day to our own. This second and non-Platonic influence leading to a stress upon purpose in Nature is nothing new, but simply the fundamental empirical tendency of Naturalism to which we have so often referred. Aristotle and a long line of his followers, especially among philosophers and biologists, have recognized purposiveness in Nature because they could not shut their eyes to it. It seemed to be there, before their faces; and as good empiricists they felt it would be disloyalty to their life-long pursuit of truth if, out of the lesser loyalty to a preconceived theory, they should deny it or seek, artificially, to explain it away.

Aristotle's universe, therefore, while material and efficient causes play their part in it,

is shot through with final causation. This is
not presented in the form of the "Design
Argument" of the eighteenth century.
Though Aristotle rejects Atomism he remains
naturalistic. The purposes he finds are not
foisted upon Nature from without. They are
immanent and form an essential element of
Nature herself. They are not presented as the
work of a Creator. For Aristotle there is no
Creator. The Cosmos is eternal. But Nature
herself—especially living Nature—is full of
unconscious, immanent purposes which steadily guide the lines of development which we
find. It was on this question of teleology more
than on any other that the two great naturalistic systems of Greece—the Aristotelian and
the Democritean—diverged. For many centuries the Aristotelian form completely dis-
placed its rival. And not without cause. For
the early form of Atomism which Leucippus
and Democritus proposed was, as I have more
than once said, too thin, too unempirical,
too naïve to express the facts of a universe,
a knowledge of whose complexity was rapidly
growing year by year. Here as so often, before and since, a crude Naturalism had to
give way before a more critical Naturalism.

The Aristotelian tendency—its system and
its growing empiricism—was the dominating

influence within Naturalism for nearly two millenniums. Aristotle had rejected Plato's rejection of Ionian science. To a considerable extent he had joined hands with the Pre-Socratic thinkers. But in his insight that science is of the universal, in his respect for the facts of life and mind as he found them, in his desire for systematic thought, he was to the end something of a Platonist. His tendency was steadily in the direction of empirical science; and the tendency continued among his followers throughout the Alexandrian period. It was, indeed, not so strong as one might have wished. Loyalty to accepted theories and to great names stood often in its way. Aristotle himself, in fact—much against what he himself would have wished—came to be, in the centuries after his death, one of the great foes to the achievement of his own dearest purposes. For so great became his authority that his tentative opinions were often accepted as indisputable facts and vetoed further investigation. Instead of looking to Nature and experience it was found much easier and more satisfying to assert that *"philosophus dixit."* An interesting example of the use of authority in place of observation during the Middle Ages among writers on Nature is found in the age-long controversy as to whether roosters come from long eggs or from round eggs. Aristotle had said that "long and pointed eggs are female: those that are round, or more rounded at the narrow end, are male." * Writers on Natural History lined up on the side of Aristotle and against him, but, apparently no one thought of hatching out a long egg and a round one to see what would happen.

For over two thousand years the question was debated with some of the greatest names in human history on one side or the other, while no effort appears to have been made to learn the truth by experiment. When finally the facts came out as a result of observation, it was all done so easily and quietly that even the names of the poultrymen who settled the mighty argument are unknown.†

The advance of Naturalism, both in antiquity, in the Middle Ages, and in modern times has been characterized by constant cooperation and struggle between the desire for system and loyalty to the empirical method. Both are absolutely essential if any knowledge of Nature, worthy of the name, is to be attained. Without keeping close to the facts

* *Historia Animalium,* 559ᵃ.
† E. Parmalee Prentice, *Farming For Famine,* p. 77.

and looking humbly to experience for them the theory of Nature becomes fantastic, dogmatic, and thin. But a mere writing down of separate facts with no construction and interrelating of them by means of hypotheses and theories would give us next to nothing at all.

Empirical discoveries are of little value in isolation. We have reason to prize them only because, on the one hand, they enable us to anticipate a larger course and order of experience, and, on the other, their bearing upon the further facts of experience brings us a better comprehension of Nature, or our total world. The growth of Naturalism has necessarily meant the amassing of larger and larger collections of facts, a more critical appraisal of the evidence, and a constantly changing arrangement of our data into more inclusive and more harmonious systems. The same story is repeated age after age. Some great mind, such as that of Aristotle, thinks together as much of the relevant data known to its generation as can be grasped, and constructs for them a nearly harmonious system. The next stage is the discovery of new facts —in part, it may be, through application of the system, in part independently of it. Usually some of these new facts fail to fit; and when, in the course of time, a considerable mass of them has accumulated, they force a modification or complete reconstruction of the system. Such a theoretical change may also be brought about by further refinements of a purely theoretical sort. Thus new philosophical constructions of the facts are built up age after age, and the doctrine of Nature becomes steadily richer in empirical content and more complex and subtle in abstract theory. So with every age a new and relatively critical and empirical Naturalism is substituted for an older Naturalism that is seen to be relatively crude and dogmatic.

It has often happened that the greatest obstacle to the advance of Naturalism has been the conservatism of the theorist and his loyalty to the Naturalism of his youth. In every field theory tends, on the one hand, to stimulate and direct empirical discovery, and, on the other, to lag behind or even to obstruct and discredit it. If the new fact is notably out of harmony with the accepted system those who believe it are damned (according to the tastes of the age) as heretical or as superstitious. Since the accepted system has been identified with science, those who accept the unexpected discoveries are plainly not true scientists, and may be burned at the stake or branded as charlatans. Thus loyalty to a past and no longer adequate Naturalism has frequently been the most venomous foe to those who would carry the banner of Naturalism to new and greater conquests.

One of the best-known instances of this oft-repeated dialectic in the development of Naturalism from systematic thesis, through empirical antithesis, to the synthesis of an enriched theory, which then becomes a new thesis to be enriched again and superseded in its turn, is to be found in the story of astronomical theory. I need only remind you of the headings of the history. How early Greek thinkers strung together the many facts concerning the motion of the heavenly bodies through the hypothesis of concentric spheres. How Eudoxus, the colleague of Plato, taking into account later and more exact observations concerning the planets, estimated the number of the spheres required for a complete explanation at twenty-two. How as a result of further calculations this number was raised by Callippus to thirty-three, and by Aristotle himself to forty-seven or possibly fifty-five. How in the following century a completely new theory was advanced by Aristarchus which substituted the sun for the earth as the center of the revolving spheres. How in a century more observation of the motions and irregularities of the sun, moon, and planets led Hipparchus—commonly considered the greatest of the ancient astronomers—to give up the heliocentric theory and put the earth back once more at the center of the universe: a conception elaborated and carried to its most finished form in the second century A.D. by the astronomer Ptolemy. And how finally the Christian Church accepted the Ptolemaic system, together with the whole Aristotelian philosophy and science. The acceptance of Aristotle was not sudden nor unmeditated. It followed only after a long struggle—a part of the famous "conflict between science and theology"—and in adopting Aristotelianism the Church brought its thought distinctly "up to date" and allied itself with the most recent and rational form of Naturalism.

But if the Church could remain satisfied with the authoritative form of Naturalism, there were some naturalists who could not. As so often before, a more critical and empirical Naturalism began to be discontented with the old and orthodox formulation. The love of system and the love of facts once more fell out, and the collection of new data threw doubt upon the old theories. The empirical discoveries of the Moslems and increased mathematical insight forced such violent al-

terations in the Aristotelian-Ptolemaic doctrine that Copernicus suggested—as a purely
mathematical possibility—the restoration of
the heliocentric theory; while Kepler gave up
the perfect circular motions of the heavenly
bodies and substituted the despised ellipse,
because the new data could not be put together on the old plan; and Galileo insisted
that the conception of the earth's motion
round the sun was not merely a mathematical
formula but represented an actual fact. In
defense of orthodox Naturalism the Church
forced Galileo to "abjure, curse, and detest"
the notion that the earth moved. "*E pur si
muove*." Recent investigators forbid us to
believe that Galileo made this famous remark.
But if he didn't he should have. In another
Italian phrase, the story that he did so, if not
vero, is *ben trovato*.

In spite of the alliance between orthodox
Naturalism and the Church, the more critical
Naturalism steadily made its way. Man's
home, the earth, was thus forced to give up
its central position in the universe, and become a mere satellite and wandering planet.
Much more important in its philosophical
implications, as Lovejoy has recently pointed
out, was another new conception of the time;
namely, that the universe was neither spheri-

cal nor of any definable shape, because it was infinite. The philosophical consequences of this astronomical discovery were realized most fully by the monk, Giordano Bruno. They fell nothing short of a transformation of man's conception of Nature and of himself. With Bruno this resulted in the rejection of the anthropomorphic conceptions of God and the world which his Church had taught him, and the substitution of a spiritual pantheism.

Thus far in dealing with the birth of modern Naturalism I have stressed chiefly the victory of the empirical method and of the newly discovered facts over the ancient naturalistic system. But system had quite as much to do with the changed conceptions which the Renaissance ushered in as had the discovery of fresh data.

Thus Bruno's picture of the infinity of worlds was largely based upon—and still more largely popularized by—a familiar and even Platonic theory: I refer to what Lovejoy has called the Principle of Plenitude: "the divine essence is infinite," hence could not be the cause of a finite effect. But the systematic conception which inspired and guided Galileo and Descartes in laying out the ground plan, so to speak, of Naturalism was something different from the thought which moved the

poetic Bruno. The new conception on which
the Cartesian world-view was built was mathematics.

This new Cartesian conception was to a
considerable degree a return to the principles
of Leucippus and Democritus. It was con-
sciously anti-Aristotelian and anti-teleologi-
cal. It meant the substitution, so far as possible, of quantity for quality, the substitution
of mechanical pushes and pulls for purpose,
the universal extension of exact measure and
number, the transformation of the entire
physical world, with its seeming but illusory
secondary qualities and final causes, into a
complete and perfect geometry. I have suggested that this conception was a return from
Aristotle to Democritus. In a sense it was
more extreme than this. It went back of
Democritus almost to Parmenides. For Descartes' ideal for the physical world was complete rationality. It should contain nothing
contingent, nothing unpredictable, no surd,
no mere datum, no merely empirical element.
It should be frozen mathematics, pure rationality. It was with this in mind that Descartes
identified matter with space, thus annexing
physics to geometry. Motion, indeed, was retained, and change; he did not go all the way
with the boldly rational Parmenides; though

how he was justified in keeping a place for change and motion in his purely rational world has never been made clear. But all motions and all changes in his world had to be entirely determined by previous motions and various mathematical laws. So true to these principles was Descartes that he properly concluded there was no reason whatever for believing the brutes to be conscious—since all their motions and seeming "expressions" were due entirely to mathematical laws and mechanical forces. All the lower animals were, therefore, quite consistently taken to be mere automata, unconscious machines, more complex, indeed, but no less purely mechanical than the lever or the pulley.

This complete mechanization of the physical world was motivated, not by empirical considerations, but by a fundamental rationalism, a conviction that the world *must be* through-and-through transparent to reason. The Cartesian Naturalism was not a collection of facts and empirical observations, but primarily a *system*. This system had in it, as we have seen, elements both Democritean and Eleatic. It also had an essentially Platonic element. If Descartes, the devout theist, had been challenged to justify his conviction that the universe actually was built on his absolutely rationalistic mathematical plan, he must have responded, had he truthfully presented his position, that things are mathematical *because this is best*. In short, his answer would have been essentially Platonic in nature, and he might well have used the identical words attributed to Socrates in the *Phaedo*, which I recently quoted.

During the course of the Renaissance the Parmenidean-Democritean-Platonic system of Descartes steadily triumphed over the Platonic-Aristotelian-Thomistic theory of the Middle Ages. What were the reasons for its victory? The triumph of the Copernican over the Ptolemaic astronomy was largely due to the discovery of new facts which were much more simply construed on the former than on the latter hypothesis. To some extent a similar explanation may be given for the success of the more general and inclusive Cartesian Naturalism over the Aristotelian Naturalism. But only to a partial extent. Descartes rested his case but slightly on empirical evidence. It was a direct comparison of the two theoretical systems rather than the question of their empirical vindication that gave the advantage to the Cartesian doctrine. For one thing, the mathematical view of the universe was perfectly consistent with a kind of general teleology. Descartes was a sincere theist and a good Catholic, and he believed that God had purposely made the best conceivable kind of world. All the teleology that liberal religion demanded was thus provided by the mechanical view. Moreover, when it came to particular processes that needed explanation, mathematical calculation brought specific enlightenment; whereas the teleological explanation, since it explained everything, really explained nothing. Thus the mechanical hypothesis provided methods for specific and practical prediction; while from the pragmatic point of view the teleological doctrine helped not at all.

Cartesian Naturalism was given its first formulation by Newton. Since Newton's time it has crowned and dominated our science like a great Church set upon a hill. New empirical facts have forced modifications of it in many details, and in recent years it has had to be patched, repaired, and repainted, and various parts of it taken down and rebuilt. Thus it has come to take on something like the appearance of a venerable cathedral begun in the Romanesque period, completed by Gothic builders, and redecorated by Baroque artists. Not a few students of physics have come to feel very suspicious of its value. Is it, perhaps, a somewhat crude and outmoded form of Naturalism? Do we need a new naturalistic system in physics? Einstein and his followers think we do. Even more fundamentally, do we need a new naturalistic philosophy? Whitehead and his followers, and many a student of Nature who is neither an Einsteinian nor a Whiteheadean think that we do. In our days, as so often before, the particular conclusion, the particular system of Naturalism is changing rapidly and may be expected to continue to change in the future. But the spirit, the aim of Naturalism, and its empirical-rational method is what it was at the beginning of human science and philosophy.

The long struggle through the ages to bring naturalistic teachings into closer and ever more exact conformity to the actualities of Nature has not been without blood and pain: Naturalism has had its martyrs. Giordano Bruno perishing amid the flames of the Camp dei Fiore in Rome was by no means unique. And aside from those who paid with their lives for their loyalty to the truth, we should not forget the many noble thinkers who have found all doors closed to them and their careers blasted because they proclaimed too soon daring conclusions which in later years all the world acclaimed as true. Their

Cassandra voices, unbelieved by their contemporaries, undistinguished by their successors, are altogether lost and forgotten except as they contribute to the profound undertone of Humanity's aspiration and steady victory through seeming defeat.

It is a mistake, however, to picture the martyrs of Naturalism as the prey of stupid or wicked anti-naturalists. It is exceedingly misleading to think of man's struggle to understand and dominate Nature as primarily "the Struggle between Science and Theology." There has, indeed, been a war and a long and fierce one; but it has been a civil war. It has been a war of system against system. But the system that most commonly has delayed the acceptance of the more critical and empirical Naturalism with its new insights has been the orthodox though relatively crude and dogmatic Naturalism already in possession of the field.

The loyal soldiers of Naturalism in its best sense who gave their careers and their blood in its service have not been the only sufferers. In looking back over three thousand years of difficult progress we must not forget the uneasiness, the heartbreak, the agony which have accompanied every substitution of the new for the old. The dear familiar Cosmos of our fathers—thus every generation living in a period of intellectual change has felt— whither is it fled? Its myths were so beautiful, its gods so kindly, the dwelling place it gave to man so comfortable. The crystalline spheres, revolving in the one perfect motion, each presided over by a pure and mighty spirit, and all animated by love for God— was it not a noble and inspiring conception?

Look how the floor of heaven
Is thick inlaid with patines of bright gold:
There's not the smallest orb which thou beholdest
But in his motion like an angel sings,
Still quiring to the young-eyed cherubims.
Such harmony is in immortal souls,
But whilst this muddy vesture of decay
Doth grossly close us in, we cannot hear it.

The music is gone now; so are the spheres; so is the comfort of the limited and shapely universe. So are the dominating spirits moving through their love for God. Instead, the uninhabited, purely material masses of matter, the crushingly unpicturable distances, the silence and the cold of the interstellar spaces. And the Kind Heavenly Father who created the world in the year 4004 B.C. for man to live in, who always answers the prayer of faith, and whose loving Providence intervenes miraculously to care for each of His children—where is He? No, the progress of Naturalism has not been accompanied by one unbroken and harmonious song of triumph and joy. One of the leading disciples of contemporary Naturalism says that our achievement, in banishing the older conceptions of Nature and substituting the modern ones, "is like climbing a high mountain and finding nothing at the top except a restaurant where they sell ginger-beer, surrounded by fog but equipped with wireless." *

There have been losses as well as gains in the steady advance of Naturalism. Yet I think there are but few of us who would seriously wish ourselves back in the good old days of particular Providences and singing spheres and anthropomorphic deities. Not only should we find life almost unendurable without the protection from disease and filth, and the many devices for human intelligent intercourse and general well-being which we owe to applied science; but, because we are men and must needs consider nothing that is human as alien to us, it would be intolerable to be limited or bound in our efforts to pierce farther and farther into the mysteries of Nature. Whether it brings comfort or pain,

* Bertrand Russell, *What I Believe*, p. 3.

the naturalistic drive can never be stopped. Because we are men, not oysters, we can never say to any passing moment or to any lovely philosophic or religious conception that pleases us, but which runs counter to reason and the facts, "*Verweile doch, du bist so schön.*" This we cannot do because we are men; and "all men by nature desire knowledge."

CHAPTER II

NATURALISM, LIFE, AND EVOLUTION

THE need to predict and the desire to understand—which we might call the two parents of natural science and of the whole study of Nature—presuppose that events are ordered. If there were no order among natural events, if there were no regularity in the relations between them, if sequences among them were never repeated, it would be alike vain to attempt to utilize the natural forces and to understand them. The notion of natural law, therefore, and of causation has always been implicit in man's thought and action as he has seriously faced Nature.

The attitude, both emotional, conative, and intelligent, which was ultimately to develop into the concept of causation had its origin, I suppose, for the race, as it has its origin still for the individual, in the double experience of successful effort on the one hand, and of defeated resistance on the other. When the child or the savage exerting his whole strength lifts a heavy weight, or is carried along against his will by stream or wind, by father or foe, he has an experience of efficient force which is *sui generis*, and which will for all his days put meaning into the concepts of cause and effect.

The notion of causation has been implicit within the pursuit we have called Naturalism from the very beginning. For a long time it was only implicit. Very primitive men were convinced that things happened because things made them happen, and many times every day they wagered their lives upon it. But the formulation of the meaning of this constraint—that was not so soon achieved. Have we, indeed, achieved it yet?

The Ionian naturalistic philosophers constantly made use of the concept, as did also Socrates and Plato, but Aristotle was the first who attempted to give an explicit account of it. And this, indeed, is saying too much: for while he distinguished material and form and purpose from what he properly called efficient cause, he took it for granted all would know, from their own experience or from his examples, what this latter meant, and made no elaborate attempt to analyze and define it. In fact, no elaborate analysis of causation and its alleged necessity was made for more than two thousand years, until David Hume challenged all comers to point out the "necessary connection" which nearly everyone before him had taken for granted. His conclusion was that causation is only a name for a fairly regular sequence of events, and that if there be any necessity in the matter this is merely the subjective necessity of habit—the queer and unjustified fact that if we have often noted B following A, we can't help expecting B whenever A appears.

Hume's analysis did not at once destroy the superstition that there is something more in the causal relation than a merely temporal sequence. The scientists took no notice of what the Scotch philosopher had said; and among the philosophers, the great German of Scotch ancestry, up in Königsberg, rushed to the defense of the venerable concept. The reality of universal and necessary connection between cause and effect, Kant insisted, is demonstrated by, because it is presupposed in, the fact of natural science and its laws, or, in other words, human knowledge. It is, therefore, not an empirical generalization but a necessary category of thought; and since causation is thus vindicated, Natural Science, with its universality and necessity, is by it saved.

Now I am aware that it is both foolhardy

and absurd to attempt the condensation of Kant's doctrine of causation within two sentences. But I also know that if I should start an adequate discussion of it with any real or imaginary Kantian, we should have to postpone the further consideration of Naturalism to the crack of doom. Hence I shall have to content myself with expressing my own opinion, with as much humility as is compatible with a dogmatic statement, but with a certain confidence because my opinion, I feel sure, is that of nearly all naturalistic thinkers. To avoid dogmatism as far as possible, let me then put it this way: that philosophers of the naturalistic school are unable to see that Kant has really answered Hume, or that Causation, as Kant believed, has saved Science; but that something nearly equivalent has happened, namely, that Science has saved Causation.

For, as we saw at the very beginning of this lecture, Science, in both its practical and its theoretical form, presupposes at least a certain amount of ascertainable order in Nature, and only so far as natural events are ordered and that order is known can we understand Nature or make use of her. Only so far as events occur in regular and ascertainable sequences can we know anything about the future or the past. Unless we can count upon some degree of regularity in the sequence of events all that we can possibly know will be the immediate data, the purely subjective content of the present, momentary consciousness. That natural events have been to some extent ordered in the past seems to be empirically very probable; but that they will be so in the future, neither empirical evidence nor *a priori* considerations can demonstrate. To believe it is a matter of faith. But it is a necessary faith. It is perhaps a leap in the dark; but if so, our only option to the leap is swift and certain death.

To say this is not to say that everything has a cause, or that necessary and invariable connection holds in every region of Reality. But if there be regions of Reality in which causal order in some sense or other fails to hold, then in *those* regions no science, no knowledge of more than the immediately given, can be. Thus causation is a necessary postulate of Naturalism. Nor has the new quantum mechanics done anything to make this less true. If it turns out to be the case that (as the Heisenberg principle asserts) it is impossible to determine at the same time the position and the velocity of a particle, that in this connection no ascertainable order can be, then this much of reality is removed from human knowledge. Possibly, as Einstein and Planck maintain, the impossibility of learning the relations here involved is due to the inevitable limitations of our techniques, remotely related to the inability of astronomy to discover the geography of the other side of the moon. Probably as Miss Stebbing insists, we are here faced with the impossibility of knowing "the initial conditions in the case of quantum phenomena." But even if the difficulty goes deeper than this, as Compton and Eddington believe, the principle of causal necessity in mass physics will be unaffected. In the relations between groups or systems of mass particles ascertainable order must hold if knowledge is to be possible; and that they do hold must, therefore, still be a postulate of Naturalism.

Hume's attack upon the concept of necessary causal connection was far from being successful; but it would be safe to say that more insight into the nature of causation has come to us, directly or indirectly, through Hume than through any other philosopher. Since his time and Kant's, moreover, philosophical students of Nature have devoted a great deal of thought to the concept of causality; and while further light and further analysis are doubtless needed, certain characteristics of the causal relation have pretty clearly emerged. The most obvious of these —the statement which goes back indeed to Hume himself—is the fact that the causal relation *is* a relation. Causation is a relation between two or more events, or aspects of events. This relation, secondly (as Hume again pointed out), is not a logical nor mathematical relation. It is not, for example, the relation of identity: for the need which forces Naturalism, and indeed man himself, to postulate causation is the need to get out of the present into the future or the past—the need to anticipate and to understand. Plainly the relation of identity can never answer that need: a present event cannot be identical with a past or future one. Nor is the causal relation of any other sort which would enable the observer of the cause to know *a priori* what the effect must be. This teaching of Hume's has been confirmed by every empirical discovery of Natural Science since his day. The causal relation is one to be learned only through experience.

A third characteristic of the causal relation—and one indeed which was implied in what has just been said—is this: that it is essentially temporal. The events within a

causal sequence have "temporal asymmetry."
Nature is not merely a collection of static
material objects, nor of purely mathematical
"values." Change is real, and change is always
in one direction. The causal relation has the
one-way character of the time-stream. Hera-
cleitus was at least as near the truth as
Parmenides. Nature is process. The causal
relation can never be reduced to a merely
functional relation.

But if causation is always a temporal relation it is never merely that. Nor is it temporal sequence many times repeated. Here
Hume was wrong, and with him one of the
Bertrand Russells—as some of the other Bertrand Russells have shown. A mere temporal
sequence, even if it occur many times, is not
what we mean by causation, nor is it the sort
of thing that Science and Naturalism postulate and must postulate. Several times every
working day the clock strikes the hour on the
campus of the University of Michigan; and
immediately the students of the University
of Indiana change classes. Here is a very regular and oft-repeated temporal sequence; but
none of the students or faculty of either university would believe a Humean who should
inform them that the Ann Arbor bell was the
cause of the rush out of and into class in

Bloomington. On the other hand a boy once and only once in his life gets a lucky opportunity to shy a rock through a plate-glass window. But all agree that the impact of the rock is the cause, or part of the cause, of the shattering of the glass.

What we mean by causation, and what we must mean, is still in need of further analysis; but at least this much seems clear. It is a relation between events, but not a merely temporal relation, nor a logical or mathematical relation, nor, for that matter, the relation of likeness or of difference. We mean by it something more like what we find in ourselves when effort produces intended results, or when we are forced to move against our will. The empirical facts and the necessary postulates of Naturalism join in indicating that Reality is full of dynamic lines of continuous influence, streaming on and crossing, conflicting, reinforcing, interweaving, in infinite variety; full of things mutually sensitive to each other, and mutually responsive; a system of interaction and of events and things mutually determined. There is no event or thing cut off from others: none that is related to others by logical relations only. Everything is what it is in part by virtue of its relation to everything else. An analysis which peels off and disregards these relations, while it may be useful for certain special purposes, must give a very partial, warped, and false view of its object. The causal influences playing upon a thing from the remote past, its own handing on of influence to other things, its coöperation, its effects, its function—these are a large part of the thing's nature. As some of these relations go far into the future, there is a sense in which an event may be said to be still acting and thus achieving a part of its character long after it seems to have ceased. The event known as Caesar's crossing the Rubicon is characterized chiefly by its relation to events that took place long after the great Julius had reached the farther bank. In so far as a cruder Naturalism of the purely mechanistic sort fails to leave room for facts of this kind, it leaves out many of the perfectly real aspects of Nature—a mistake easily avoided by a more critical Naturalism. The causal stream is thus, as Professor Swabey has so well expressed it, "a perpetual creativity." It is

an everlasting going on from one condition to another. Causation is the very essence of nature, dynamic and creative, "forever flaring up and dying down," the separate strands of which we attempt to isolate intellectually in our laws.

In itself it is pure production, an inner necessity by which nature unfolds from stage to stage or else descends in the direction of chaotic homogeneity. It is something which we can understand only by a direct apprehension, for we cannot reduce it to anything else; rather all particular processes are mere instances of the universal creativeness. We know what it is, for, in our voluntary action, the stream of universal causation flows through the channels of our will and our voluntary actions are true causes as well as true effects.*

From considerations such as these there emerges a conception of the universe, of the totality of Nature, as an almost organic whole. As Aristotle, the great naturalist, said long ago: "All things in the Universe are somehow ordered together, whatever swims in the sea or flies in the air or grows on the earth, nothing exists apart from and without some kind of relation to the rest." † "The smallest candle fills a mile with its rays, and the papillae of a man run out to every star." ‡

The reality of the causal relation, as we have seen, is fundamental to Naturalism, and I do not see how the naturalistic philosopher can think out the meaning of causation with-

* *Being and Being Known,* p. 197.
† *Metaphysics X,* 1075^a.
‡ Emerson, *Conduct of Life,* p. 42.

out, in the end, coming to some such conclusion as that suggested. This conception of Nature as an infinitely rich and inwardly unitary whole will have its important bearings upon naturalistic views in every department of Reality. And upon none more obviously than upon the living world of plant and animal and human life. Here as elsewhere we shall find the familiar contrast between a crude and a critical Naturalism, between a less and a more empirical and inclusive view of Nature.

The problem which faces Naturalism in the realm of the biological is, of course, the understanding of living Nature, the explanation of the peculiar facts of life. "Explanation" I am here using in a large sense: in the sense that means the placing of the facts in relation to all relevant facts in such fashion that they will throw light upon each other, that they will fall into an order, into a unity, so that we shall have, not a heterogeneous chaos, but a luminous whole.

Systematic description is the first step toward such understanding and explanation, and the beginning of this (as of so many other scientific undertakings) was made by Aristotle. Little of a really scientific sort was added to Aristotle's achievement till the Renaissance. With the rise of Cartesianism something had to be done about living forms and their seemingly orderless activities: and they were brought under the general rationalistic formula for all physical entities by Descartes' special theories that the animals, like the vegetables, were mere automata; that they were entirely unconscious; and that all vital processes were mere cases of the phenomena studied by physics and ultimately reducible to geometry plus the laws of motion. A dictum of this sort, unsupported by careful empirical investigation, may be a brilliant hypothesis of a prophetic genius, but taken as serious science or philosophy it is a good example of what I have called crude Naturalism. It needed a great amount of critical and experimental analysis; and this it has received in the three centuries since Descartes' time.

The central question for biological Naturalism during these centuries, however, has not been whether animals are automata, but the larger inquiry how these infinitely varied and most curiously interrelated organic forms are to be explained. The theologians had their answer: all living things were made by God in the year 4004 B.C., and if one doubted it, the many "marks of design" were furnished in immeasurable lectures and books. And it was not only the theologians who were satisfied with the traditional view. The greatest biologist of his day, Linnaeus, held with Aristotle that species never change, and, with the orthodox and the deist, that all the species were created by God in their present form at about the date named.

But the naturalistic thinkers who followed Linnaeus were not satisfied with so perfect an explanation and insisted upon looking for finite causes which would illuminate the organic world from within. Among the first to suggest an explanation scientific in form was Lamarck who in the early years of the nineteenth century put forward the hypothesis that the direct effect of the environment upon individual organisms, and their reactions to it—notably "use and disuse" of organs—produced changes in them, and that these changes were inherited by their descendants, and thus new varieties and new species arose. Before this theory could be thoroughly tested, Darwin brought forward his great hypothesis of Natural Selection. Both Darwinism and Lamarckianism were sternly rejected, not only by the theologians, who appealed to the Book of Genesis, but by nearly all the older defenders of Naturalism, who appealed to Aristotle. Half a century of warfare followed,

but the cruder and outmoded Naturalism
was at last defeated by the more critical
and more thoroughly empirical hypothesis, and Natural Selection, with its subordi-
nate theories of the Struggle for Existence,
Sexual Selection, Protective Coloring, etc.,
was accepted not only by nearly all biologists,
but (perhaps even more enthusiastically) by
nearly all really up-to-date theological semi-
naries and liberal clergymen. There was one
thing settled at last and for keeps! But alas,
within the memory of most of us, even this
rock of theoretical solidity was proved not
immune to the attacks of radical Naturalism.
One would hardly anticipate danger to the
Gibraltar of Darwinism from so innocent a
thing as a primrose by the river's brim. But
others besides Peter Bell have been mistaken
in thinking a primrose to be just a primrose
and nothing more. In the hands of DeVries
it proved a kind of bomb which forced a very
considerable reconstruction of the Darwinian
theory. Worse was to come. It is now seriously doubted whether the Struggle for Existence has more than a slight effect upon
Natural Selection: Sexual Selection has been
nearly given up: and Protective Coloring no
longer protects. Natural Selection has indeed
been retained as an important influence in

evolution, but in order to be retained it has
had to be reinforced and therefore again modified by the new genetic theory deriving from
Mendel's investigations. Bringing together
the biological data at hand in the first years
of this century, and leaning especially upon
the recent investigations into the germ cell,
Weismann constructed a Neo-Darwinism. Up
to a very few years ago his theories were accepted by orthodox Darwinians as the last
word on evolution; but the most distinctive
and original of them are now going the way
of all flesh. But the chief influence in throw-
ing the Natural Selection theory into the
background was the gradual realization that
while it doubtless is a true theory so far as it
goes, it fails to answer the crucial question
concerning the causality at work in evolution.
Darwin himself saw this deficiency, but the
first to say much about it were not the biologists but the theologians. Darwinism, it came
to be realized, gave a partial explanation of
the non-survival of the "unfit," but told us
nothing of the arrival of the "fit." And this,
after all, is the central question. Darwin had
propounded it in the title of his great book
—*The Origin of Species*—but had not even
attempted the answer. We know why some

species and varieties die out, but what is the
source of variations?

To be as brief about it as one may, biologists are divided on this crucial issue into
three schools known respectively as Mechanism, Neo-Lamarckianism, and Vitalism. The
theory called Mechanism maintains that the
rise of variations and their stabilization and
continuation through heredity has to be entirely explained, in the last analysis, by appeal to the same laws, forces, and qualities of
matter with which physics and chemistry deal.
In a sense, of course, this theory is as old
and time-worn as Ionian Materialism, but in
the hands of the trained biologists of our day
it is an up-to-date, well-considered, and per-
suasive doctrine. It has absorbed Neo-Darwinism and Natural Selection, DeVries and
the mutation theory, Mendel and the newly
discovered genes. It is strong in both experimental evidence and logical analysis.

More specifically the mechanistic view
maintains that the origin of mutations,
whether great or slight, is to be found either
in new combinations of the genes or in purely
chance chemical changes within some of them.
Not often are specific suggestions made as
to the course of this development, but occa-

sionally they are. Thus Professor Shull proposes that evolution started with individual genes, which came to unite in various chance ways. Some early mutations were produced by chemical changes in the molecules. The stability needed for the development of species was furnished by mitosis, or cell division; the recombination by biparental reproduction; further variation by the inherited capacity of meiosis, or the specialization of germ cells; and further stability by the grouping of the genes into chromosomes. Given this equipment, plus the implied character of heredity, the production of new species and the stability of old ones can be explained without appeal either to Lamarckian influences from outside, or vitalistic influences from behind. Such is Shull's theory. Other mechanists might suggest other hypotheses, but the general principle of determination by the purely physical and chemical would be the same.

In favor of the mechanistic hypothesis are two types of consideration; one empirical, the other methodological. Careful observation of actual mutations shows the truth of the general genetic theory on its positive side, and though it by no means as yet explains all the facts of evolution, it has made such progress in the last forty years that one may question whether it be not almost foolhardy to set any limit to its possible advance. Since, moreover, there must have been a time when life began, it seems at least extremely probable that life arose out of the inorganic. The other type of argument, as I have said, is based upon the demands of scientific method. It consists in an attempt to show that the opponents of Mechanism are committed to principles that are essentially unscientific and which make exact knowledge impossible.

The other theories, in their turn, are like Mechanism in finding, perhaps, their strongest arguments in the weak points of their opponents. Against Mechanism in particular a number of considerations are urged, of which the best known is the very great difference between living organisms and inorganic matter, between the laws of life and the laws of the merely physical and chemical. No one denies that physical and chemical laws hold for living as they do for non-living matter. But in plants and animals there so obviously is something additional, and this addition is so strikingly new in kind, that he who does not recognize it would seem to be either hopelessly prejudiced in advance, or else so insensitive as to be constitutionally incapacitated for any kind of scientific observation. And not only is this enormous contrast plain in a general way: it becomes even more striking when one considers specific characteristics and powers possessed by living things. Driesch's well-known experiments will here recur to your minds—experiments such as those on the regeneration of organs, and the development of a whole organism from merely a fraction of the embryo. As Driesch points out, it is really impossible to imagine any kind of machine, or any combination of chemical elements, which could achieve this. Professor Wolff's experiment with regeneration in the salamander is perhaps less well known but equally striking. He removed the lens from the salamander's eye and a new lens grew and took its place. This new lens was produced not from the ectodermal part of the skin (the normal source of the lens, from which the first lens had grown), but from a part of the iris which comes from a region of the brain in the embryo. The iris had not been injured in the removal of the first lens; the new lens, that is, did not grow out of a wound in the iris, for there was no wound. The stimulus to this new growth from the iris was not to be found in anything that happened to the iris but in what happened to

another part of the eye. It was not the iris so
much as the organism as a whole that responded: and it responded to the new need of
sight by growing a new lens from the iris. It
would be obviously vain to seek an explanation for this in an inherited tendency within
the genes to grow new lenses from the iris
when old lenses are lost, for such a loss never
comes about in the course of nature. Nor, for
obvious reasons, can Natural Selection throw
any light upon such a case of regeneration.
To be sure, many cases of regeneration have
been observed that show no obvious utility.
But the fact that Nature does many useless
things does not remove the seeming need of
something more than physics and chemistry
provide if we are to comprehend such facts
as those referred to.

But if the production of a new lens or a
new paw seems to demand something more
than the inorganic can by itself supply, what
shall we say of the production of mind—of
sense-perception, emotion, reason, volition,
self-consciousness? The relation of mind and
body we shall consider at some length in our
next lecture, but the mind is a part of life,
and its rise has so obvious and crucial a bearing upon the attempt to explain all of life

by physical and chemical principles that we should have no right to pass it by in this lecture without notice.

Our mental life is the only thing we know with immediate directness; the only one we cannot doubt. How about the genes? They constitute Mechanism's favorite means of explanation for the whole of evolution from the simplest protozoan to the loftiest man. Has anyone ever seen a gene? The answer to this question, I believe, is fairly definite. One or two think they have; nearly all experimenters are sure they have not. Some time ago a few biologists had the temerity to raise the disquieting question whether there are any such things. And in March, 1938, Professor Goldsmith of the University of California published a paper in the *Scientific Monthly* in which he came to the definite conclusion that the genes, upon which so much has been built, are purely imaginary and do not exist at all. Instead there are "only points, loci, in a chromosome which have to be arranged in the proper order or pattern to control normal development." *

When doctors disagree what shall the poor philosopher do? Personally I am willing to believe in the genes or not to believe in them,

* "The Theory of the Gene," *Scientific Monthly,* XLVI (March, 1938), 271.

and in general quite docilely to do as I am told whenever the doctors shall come to an agreement. But whatever the outcome, it is perfectly plain that our knowledge of the genes, or of whatever substitutes shall be proposed for them, consists, and will consist, only of probable hypotheses. Such knowledge is working well, and by the use of it valuable practical and theoretical information is steadily being secured. But after all, as I have said, our knowledge of the genes, or of the loci which Goldsmith proposes in their place, is still, and very likely always will be, of the hypothetical sort. We deal with these constructs by faith, not by sight. They are as much an invention of the scientific imagination as is Driesch's "entelechy." It is perfectly conceivable that a new theory of heredity may be published tomorrow quite as complete and quite as empirically based as the gene theory, and that in a very few years the genes will join coloric, phlogiston, and animal spirits, *mana* and other scientific myths into that land from whose bourne no traveller returns. The gene theory may be true—personally I think that it or something like it probably is true: but let us be clear that "genes," "loci," and their functions have been invented *ad hoc* for the sake of explanation, and that our knowledge of them is, to say the least, very secondary compared with our knowledge of our consciousness and ourselves. It is the mind and its activities and not the genes that constitute the primary and solid fact.

The first form of Darwinism took it for granted that the variations upon which Natural Selection works, since they are the product of chance, are rather evenly divided between all possible directions. The facts as now known do not bear out this supposition. As Shull, the able mechanist to whom I have already referred, writes: "There are many things which indicate that in the dealing out of mutations the cards are stacked. The available evidence goes to show that there are numerous restrictions upon the process of modification." Both the evidence of the very ancient world, as furnished us by geology, and the researchers of contemporary geneticists show us that the evolution of changing forms usually follows fairly regular lines of direction. Thus not only the origin of mutations in general, but the direction of their course, the cumulative production of similar mutations, generation after generation, is a problem that calls for solution. "Chance" is no explanation, but a name for our ignorance, and chance cannot explain persistence of direction. Nor, as Bergson has pointed out, can Natural Selection. The early development of a new organ is usually so gradual that for many generations after its incipient appearance it can hardly affect either lethal selection or rate of reproduction in the species. It looks very much as if a new influence in addition to physical and chemical substances and forces were here at work.

If in reply it be suggested that we have no idea how wonderful the genes may be, we can but assent. In fact they must be so wonderfully different from any known combination of the matter and forces of physics and chemistry as to make the mechanists' interpretation of them almost ludicrous. A similar consideration will be suggested as to the changes in the genes, to which mutations are sometimes attributed. There can be little doubt that the genes have often changed: but how account for these changes? Shull may be correct in his hypothesis, referred to a few pages back, as to the way in which the various evolutionary stages came about—viz., through the activity of genes that possessed—or acquired—the power of handing on the character of heredity, the powers of mitosis and meiosis, of biparental reproduction and of the formation of chromosomes and of "cross-ing over" and the rest. But whence these characters and powers? And will the chemists acquiescently help us out if we try to "pass the buck" to them?

I should hasten to say that many mecha-nists have their answer and it is a perfectly definite and a decidedly good one. Their crit-ics, they will assert, have set up a man of straw and have completely misrepresented their real meaning. Mechanism does not hold that matter and physical energy, as known and analyzed by the physical sciences, can account for the facts of life. No one any longer holds, as Liebig and Laplace and Huxley did, that organic phenomena could be deduced from or predicted from or ex-plained by properties and processes of atoms and molecules. "Mechanists admit that in biology we have to deal with another element besides chemistry or molecular structure. This is variously called form, organization, or structure. Even as extreme a mechanist as Loeb insists that 'without a structure in the egg to begin with no formation of a com-plicated organism is imaginable.' " * "No gene ever does anything by itself," writes

* Cohen, *Reason and Nature,* pp. 241, 272. See also Loeb, *The Organism As a Whole,* Chaps. II, VI.

Shull: "its activities are all cooperative." *
In other words, biological, as distinct from
physical, phenomena are due not to the mechanical or chemical activity of the genes as
separate physical things, but to the coöperation, the unified action, of all, or a considerable part, of the organism. How coöperative
and unified activity is to be explained is not
suggested, but the mechanists seem to ac-
knowledge that it is not to be explained by the
inorganic. Similarly we are never told what
the needed "other element besides chemistry
or molecular structures" may be. Loeb, as we
have seen, refers to it as "structure." Cohen,
interpreting Naturalism, adds the synonyms,
"form, or organization," and refers to it as
a needed "additional category": for "the
older and simpler ideas of physics and chemistry will never be adequate for biology." †
This "additional category" can hardly be
physical or chemical. We seem, therefore, to
be left with the conclusion that Mechanism
does not really mean to be mechanical but
needs to appeal to something non-mechanical
—something which its upholders have left
about as vague as are the "principles" of
Vitalism—and perhaps not very different.

* *Op. cit.*, p. 110.
† *Op. cit.*, p. 273.

Before taking up Vitalism let me say a few words concerning the second of the three schools, referred to some pages back, that have suggestions to make concerning the origin of variations—namely, Neo-Lamarckianism. Contemporary followers of Lamarck agree with him in holding that acquired characters may be transmitted, but differ from him upon the chief source of these new characters. His stress was upon the changes in the individual's characters produced by the activity of the organisms, or lack of it—upon "use and disuse." That these may have some influence the Neo-Lamarckians believe, but their principal emphasis is upon the influence of the environment. Changes produced in the soma by the environment may, in their opinion, be transmitted and become hereditary, being handed on among the descendants long after the environmental influence that first produced it has ceased to act. Plainly if this is the case this method of producing mutations might at times result in the production of new species. The Neo-Lamarckians have adopted into their theory all that is known concerning chromosomes and genes, and are quite agreed that hereditary characters are transmitted from the germ cells only, but insist that changes within the germ cells may

be, and often are, produced by changes within
the soma.

The objections to this view, when it is put
in this rather modest form, do not seem star-
tling. There is a great deal of experimental
evidence that environmental influences produce changes which appear (after the influence has ceased) in the second and third and
later generations. The natural conclusion
from these facts would seem to be the admission of the occasional influence of the soma
upon the germ cells. The attempt is sometimes made to avoid this admission by the
theory known as parallel induction: but this
theory has so little evidence in its favor, and
is so obviously a desperate attempt to save
an outmoded hypothesis, that it is not impressive.

But to grant that characters acquired by
the soma through the influence of the environment may be transmitted is not to grant
a great deal, nor does it go very far to determining all the forces, nor the principal ones,
that determine evolutionary development.
For the Neo-Lamarckian, like the mechanist,
must presuppose the unique nature of life
and the unique characters and powers of the
genes. Such things as the transmission of the
hereditary tendency, and other potentialities

which the mechanistic theory could not explain by chemical action, are no more easily to be explained by the influence of the environment and of the soma. Both physical and chemical laws and somatic and environmental influences doubtless have their effect: but a power or character of a different category is plainly needed. Mechanism, even when supplemented by Neo-Lamarckianism, cannot explain the actual facts of development.

This new category, this "something more," is pretty evidently to be sought in the character of living matter and the processes of life. The belief in such a character, and the attempt to find or formulate it, is the one thing common to those various groups of biologists and of philosophers who are commonly lumped together under the term "Vitalism." They differ among themselves in several ways, but they are united in the conviction that there is a tendency or force other than the physical and chemical, which makes at least some slight contribution toward carrying on and directing the biological activities of the organism and the course of racial evolution.

In some ways, it must be said at the outset, this theory does not improve upon acquaintance. The evidence and the specific arguments in its favor are many, but they really amount to little more than pointing out the weaknesses of rival theories. These we have, in a general way, already considered, and in addition to them there is little or nothing of a positive sort to urge in favor of Vitalism. It has, moreover, like the other theories, certain weaknesses of its own—or rather one weakness which to the scientific mind is very serious. This is its inability to define exactly or exhibit specifically the power, character, or principle which it proposes as the needed supplement to physical and chemical laws: and consequently it seems to veto any advance in exact knowledge of an explanatory sort, for its added principles of explanation are neither quantitative nor measurable. As Cohen says:

While these principles all function as if they were psychological, they are not directly knowable either subjectively or objectively. They are entities invented to explain life, but no definite laws or phenomena are really deduced from them, any more than from the "dormitive principles" of opium in Molière's caricature of scholasticism. These vital principles serve only as sign-posts to emphasize the undoubted fact that the phenomena of life are different from those of non-living nature.*

The vitalist will respond that not all scientific explanations are in terms of the visible, tangible, and spatial. Introspective psychology—as well as all of practical thinking—makes use of conscious states, and notably of purpose, in the explanation of the activities of the human body. And are not "energy," "force," "gravity," and "magnetism," which physics appeals to repeatedly, just as invisible and intangible as Driesch's "entelechy," Reinke's "determinants," or Bergson's "*élan vital*"? Newton seems clearly to have considered force, not as the change of momentum, but as the *cause* of such change. For him, and for most physicists who are not adherents of the positivist philosophy, force was *measured* by mass times acceleration, but was not to be identified with them. For those naturalists who are not positivists, is not energy as real a part of Nature as matter, and is it not used quite as often in explanation of events in macroscopic physics? And does it not stand upon pretty much the same level as the "life force" or whatever else we may call the "something more" which even the mechanists

* *Reason and Nature,* pp. 253–254.

dimly recognize as needed for a complete explanation of organic Nature? The vitalist finds, in the individual organism and the development of the race, changes and directions which, in his opinion, Mechanism can never explain. These, therefore, seem to him to point to an additional stimulating and guiding force. Why, he asks, is not this good methodology?

It would be better methodology, as we have pointed out, if he could or would give us some more specific indication of the nature of the additional force to which he appeals. Some vitalists do this, and suggest that the vital principle needed is to be interpreted as some kind of purpose or intention. And this, perhaps, may somewhat remedy the unfortunate indefiniteness of other vitalistic theories. But we must remember that the actual influence of purpose upon action even within human life cannot be taken for granted and has not as yet entered into our discussion. Moreover, the critic of Vitalism may well ask what is this hypothetical purpose within life, and raise the question whether we should be justified by the facts in recognizing its actuality.

There are many, both within and without the vitalist school, who would answer this last question in the affirmative. John Stuart

Mill insisted that the existence of purpose in many bodily structures and processes was the necessary conclusion from a perfectly good inductive argument. Take the eye for example.

The parts of which the eye is composed, and the collocations which constitute the arrangement of those parts, resemble one another in this very remarkable property, that they all conduce to enabling the animal to see. These things being as they are, the animal sees: if any one of them were different from what it is, the animal, for the most part, would either not see, or would not see equally well. And this is the only marked resemblance that we can trace among the different parts of this structure, beyond the general likeness of composition and organization which exists among all other parts of the animal. Now the particular combination of organic elements called an eye had, in every instance, a beginning in time and must therefore have been brought together by a cause or causes. The number of instances is immeasurably greater than is, by the principles of inductive logic, required for the exclusion of a random concurrence of independent causes, or speaking technically, for the elimination of chance. We are therefore warranted by the canons of induction in concluding that what brought all these elements together was some cause common to them all; and inasmuch as the elements agree in the single circumstance of conspiring to produce sight, there must be some connection by way of causation between the cause which brought those elements together, and the fact of sight.*

The biologist Gustav Wolff, in his *Leben und Erkennen* (München, 1933), considers purposiveness in the organism even more directly visible. Our conviction that purpose has had to do with the formation of an organ, like our conviction that it has had to do with the making of a machine, is, he insists, a matter not of indirect but of immediate inference. Organic functions can, indeed, be described in purely chemical and physical terms, but even when these descriptions are complete we are aware of an unexplained remainder. This unexplained remainder is not a gap or a missing link: it is a character of the whole. An organism, in short, is seen at once to possess what Wolff calls a *"Zielursächlichkeit oder Zweckmässigkeit"*—a character which one sees also in machines, but which is possessed by no merely natural inorganic thing. It may be said that this is Paley with his watch all over again: and so indeed it is. But old-fashioned as Paley may appear and ridiculed

* *Three Essays on Religion,* pp. 170–171.

as he often is, one may still query whether a satisfactory answer has ever been given to his fundamental assertion of the obvious teleology of such a thing as a watch or an eye.

The attempt to come to some conclusion on the controversy between Mechanism, Neo-Lamarckianism, and Vitalism is, for the outsider at any rate, a peculiarly baffling experience. And, indeed, one may question whether the outsider—and I mean by that term the mere philosopher—has here any right to an opinion. I confess to a considerable amount of sympathy with the technical biologist when he writes: "By patience and industry and intelligence, biologists hope to advance their work. But so long as they have not found convincing evidence, it is an 'open season' for philosophers, who are too impatient to wait, but must add the biological field to their speculations." * It is doubtless true that philosophers are an impatient lot. But while the patient biologists are advancing their work through slow and solid industry, and while "they have not found any convincing evidence," philosophers can hardly be expected to cease speculating. In fact speculate they must, and they have a good

* T. H. Morgan, *The Scientific Basis of Evolution*, p. 239.

right, a real duty to do so. For the evolutionary problem, although so largely biological, is not merely biological: and the naturalistic philosopher can hardly fail to be intensely interested in the matter. And since he views the problem from a little distance, with a larger perspective than the experimentalist in the midst of the controversy can enjoy, his more objective and philosophic opinion may not be entirely worthless. As a matter of fact, naturalistic philosophers are divided upon the question, some favoring Mechanism, some favoring Vitalism as reinforced by Neo-Lamarckianism, and some feeling, as perhaps many of you do by this time, that probably all three schools are wrong. A more justifiable conclusion would be that all three schools are in part right, and that each has its contribution to make. The desideratum is, perhaps, such a combination of the essential thought of all as will give a concept of Nature that will not need to appeal to anything beyond Nature and yet will be able to include all the facts of life and mind.

Whether wrong or right, each of the three schools, at any rate, is upholding a perfectly genuine form of Naturalism. Mechanism may be quite incapable of offering an adequate

explanation of the most important facts of
life and evolution, but its aim and its method
and its aspiration, when not dogmatic, are
thoroughly naturalistic. The imponderable
influences which Vitalism believes are needed
to explain the facts may not be of the sort
that naturalists, brought up with ideas derived from chemistry, prefer. But it is at
least conceivable that the Vitalists are right:
and if they are Naturalism will just have to
accept the fact. The discovery that this is
the case would not destroy Naturalism—the
rational and empirical investigation of Nature. Whatever Nature is and however it is
dominated and guided, the naturalist will
want to find out the truth about it. No empirical discoveries, no rational conclusions
whether in favor of Mechanism or against it,
can ever be fatal to Naturalism or even
slightly harmful to it. One thing only would
be fatal to Naturalism: and that is the adop-
tion of a non-empirical point of view, the
prejudging of the question, the dogmatic
formation of a definite conclusion before or
against the evidence.

If I may venture at this point to express
a tentative opinion of my own for what it
may be worth, I shall have to confess that,

when I look in synoptic fashion at the entire
problem of living things, the characters of
individual organisms, and the whole story of
their evolution, I find it impossible to avoid
the impression of general persistent tendencies inexplicable by any imaginable kind of
merely mechanically caused process. And if
I try to satisfy myself with a purely "mechanical" solution, I find that the word has
burst its bounds, and has taken on meanings
utterly inapplicable to its literal or usual
significance. As some of the mechanists themselves admit, "something more" is needed.
And this "something more," if it is to be
serviceable for our problem, must include
within it some form of teleology. This teleology need not be—and indeed from my point
of view cannot be—a kind of external purpose, forced from without upon living things
by some anthropomorphic Creator or Artifi-
cer. The facts of life and of evolution suggest rather—and I think rather plainly point
to—some form of immanent but dynamic
teleology. This does not mean a complete acceptance of any of the present vitalistic
theories as they stand. Bergson's conception
of a creative impulse—perhaps the most
plausible of the vitalistic hypotheses—has

properly a great appeal. But, as Professor Eldridge has pointed out,* in its present form it is almost incredible since it seems to attribute to the vital impetus at the very beginning a knowledge of the various situations which each species was destined to meet. Such a vitalistic scheme—indeed every vitalistic scheme—seems plainly to need supplementation from Neo-Lamarckianism: as of course it needs constant supplementation from Mechanism. If (as I have suggested) we are to accept an immanent teleological trend or urge in the development of living forms, we cannot put all of its directive control back at some remote period of the past, but must recognize its latent wisdom (if one may so speak) continuing on at every turn, adopting the particular tendencies of its general forward movement to every new situation as it arises. If the *élan vital* is ever wise, it is always wise.

But while purely physical and chemical forces are—and presumably always will be—inadequate to the complete explanation of life and evolution, it must never be forgotten that they must furnish a very large part of it. Though they may need reinforcement from a "something more," they never cease to hold.

* *The Organization of Life,* pp. 401–414.

And the large role they play in the direction of life is not confined to the genes, or to the whole of organic matter, but is to be sought also in the inorganic environment. Life cannot be cut off from its setting with a hatchet. "The fitness of the environment" is one of the facts to be taken into consideration, if not by natural science, at any rate by naturalistic philosophy. The lines of causal continuity and influence referred to in the early part of this lecture run without break from the inorganic to the organic and back again. And it seems likely enough that if there be immanent teleology in the living world, it will be found also in the non-living. However this may be, it at least suggests the question of "emergent evolution," to which at least some brief reference should be made before the close of this lecture.

The conception of a gradual cosmic development from the simplest physical combinations and laws to the highest achievements of life and mind has been a common conception for many years. It was worked out in the middle of the last century in considerable detail by the naturalistic philosopher Herbert Spencer and by the theologian Mark Hopkins. In very recent years this idea has been rephrased and brought up to date, so

to speak, by several writers, notably by four
naturalistic thinkers—Lloyd Morgan, S.
Alexander, J. C. Smuts, and R. W. Sellars.
The name suggested for the theory by Lloyd
Morgan—emergent evolution—is the one that
has stuck. The conception is that evolution
is not confined to the organic world, but is
found also in the inorganic: and is to be seen
wherever a new combination of two or more
familiar substances or powers yields a character which could not have been predicted by
means of all that had been previously known
of the elementary substances separately.
Thus when hydrogen and oxygen are united
we have a new form of material, water, some
of whose characters had never been guessed
and never could have been guessed by examination of hydrogen and oxygen in isolation. The development of life out of the
inorganic (so the theory continues), sensation and impulse out of life, and of the
higher mental powers out of sensation and
impulse, is the same sort of thing as the development of water out of its two elements.
The laws of the lower levels remain as dominant as ever even on the higher levels, but
additive qualities emerge which had been unpredictable from the old laws.

As McDougall * and Shull † have pointed out, it is highly questionable whether in the inorganic realm we find anything that can properly be called evolution, or the production of the new. When the emergent evolutionist tells us that the qualities of water are not predictable from what is known of hydrogen and oxygen by themselves, the meaning of the assertion is ambiguous. For what *is* known about hydrogen and oxygen, or any other elements, *by themselves?* Very nearly nothing, I should suppose. Chemical knowledge, like other scientific knowledge, is "knowledge about": it is knowledge of relational qualities. An important part of our knowledge about oxygen consists in knowing what it does when combined with hydrogen. Hence either we know practically nothing about hydrogen and oxygen "by themselves" (for the reason that there is practically nothing to know), in which case it is not very significant that we could not predict the qualities of water; or else in our knowledge of hydrogen and oxygen were included the facts of what they do when combined. Noth-

* *Modern Materialism and Emergent Evolution,* Chaps. V, VI.
† *Evolution,* Chap. XVIII.

ing new in any sense scientifically important emerges in combinations of the inorganic. All that is new, in such a situation, is either (1) a new relation between old elements, or (2) a new type of experience in a conscious observer. This second is really new, but, it will be noted, its emergence is within the realm of *mind, not* in the inorganic realm. The attempt to subsume the emergence of genuinely and importantly new kinds of being, such as we find in life and consciousness, under the same category as the emergence of water from its two constituent elements is really vain.

Nor has anything been said by the disciples of emergence to show that life and mind are merely new combinations of old elements and *in that sense* emerge from the physical and chemical. If "emergent evolution" is proposed as an explanation of the higher out of the lower, of life and mind out of what we might call the mechanical, it has as yet completely failed.

On the other hand, there can be no doubt that physical and chemical substances and their laws form a part of the explanation of life and mind: doubtless "something more" is needed for a complete explanation, but physics and chemistry make their large contribution. Chronologically speaking, it is pretty plain that life did (and may again) emerge from the inorganic: and mind from the living. Such chronological relation should, and usually does, put us on enquiry whether this chronological sequence be not indicative of a causal sequence. The sequence of the genuinely new upon the old and different could not, indeed, be considered causal if we retained the scholastic maxim that "there cannot be more in the effect than there is in the cause." But, as Lovejoy has shown, there is really little or nothing to be said in defense of this maxim.* And certainly the conception of causality presented in the earlier part of this lecture is perfectly consistent with the view that there are lines of continuous influence flowing from the inorganic into the organic and the mental.

While emergent evolution, therefore, cannot explain the living and conscious in mechanistic fashion, or purely by the laws of physics and chemistry, it can give us a description, a picture, of the actual forward movement of cosmic forces and thus unite in one whole the inorganic with the organic, making of them one universe. A conception of this sort, while far from being mechanistic,

* "The Meaning of Emergence and Its Modes," *Proc. of the VI Internat. Congress of Phil.,* pp. 20–23.

would still be naturalistic, and offers an inviting field for the thought of a critical Naturalism.

Or, to picture the situation in another way, let us put together the following considerations: (1) The conception of causality proposed in the early part of this lecture—lines of continuous influence and tendency, binding together all parts of the universe; every single thing in it sensitive to and influenced by everything else; tides responding to the distant moon, disturbances in the sun affecting our terrestrial weather, light rushing from star to star, gravity binding together the most distant outskirts of the material universe; so that the Cosmos as a whole has a kind of unity, in its bewildering variety, which almost deserves the name organic. (2) The plainly teleological nature of a host of phenomena within individual organisms: the steady and persistent tendencies in the evolution of species; the accumulation of mutations in continuous lines; the direct response of organisms to changes in the environment; the inability of mechanical forces and of Natural Selection combined to account for these facts—the unity, therefore, with which both ontogeny and phylogeny point to the presence of some imponderable and seemingly teleological guidance. (3) The tendency and direction of the universe—physical, organic, psychical—toward the building up of larger, more complex, and more inwardly unitary wholes, and the emergence of higher levels of being. If the naturalistic philosopher who wants to understand Nature, and who knows he cannot really understand any of it without some kind of comprehension of all of it, who cannot satisfy himself with a crude Naturalism which leaves out of account some of the more significant facts, or which starts with some *a priori* prejudice, but who insists upon going on to a more critical and synoptic view of Nature as a whole—if, I say, such a thinker puts together the three groups of facts suggested above, he will, I believe, draw from them a very definite impression of the universe as an almost organic being, dominated, at least in part, by definite tendencies of immanent purpose.

Whatever one may think of the probable truth or persuasiveness of such an hypothesis, it is at any rate a thoroughly naturalistic one. It aims solely at learning the truth about Nature; it appeals to nothing outside of Nature but looks for its explanations to nothing but Nature itself; it stands ready to change its hypothesis at any moment if the facts demand it; and, meanwhile, it bases its tentative conclusions solely upon reason and empirical evidence.

The hypothesis is at least logically self-consistent, and is harmonious with what appears at the present to be a vast accumulation of facts. But this acceptability hinges largely upon one crucial question which we have not as yet seriously considered: the question, namely, whether purpose is ever actually efficient in the world of existent, physical things which Naturalism studies. This question we must postpone to our next lecture.

CHAPTER III

NATURALISM AND MIND

THE realm of mind was one of the last for Naturalism to enter. General outlines of order in a physical world were obvious enough, and a little study of unconscious vital phenomena brought to light many important sequences that could be counted on. But the minds of the higher animals—how mysterious they are! The thoughts and motives and future decisions of one's fellows—how hidden and how incalculable! To be sure, from very early human times there must have been certain clever individuals who possessed what today we should call a "knowledge of human nature." But not even the wisest could explain men's thoughts with certainty or predict their acts with security. Outside of the most ordinary routine of instinctive and habitual behavior, how much was to be found in the acts of others and in one's own experience that was simply incalculable and inexplicable! No wonder that the learned men of many a primitive society based their attempted explanations on magic or on possession by evil spirits.

Another hindrance in the way of even the beginnings of a scientific treatment of mind was the very vague distinction between mind and body. It was presumably a long time before there was any notion of consciousness as distinct from the body, while the subject (as we should say) of sensation and thought, the maker of decisions, was either roughly identified with the body or pictured as a kind of secondary body composed of a different kind of matter. This matter was very tenuous, indeed, and usually invisible, but it was matter none the less. Yet, though this spirit or double was matter, it did not seem to be subject to the laws of ordinary matter which observation of the physical world was beginning roughly to formulate.

To conceive of this material double was at least the beginning of serious thought on the nature of the mind. It was at least something that a distinction of some sort had been made between the visible and tangible body of a man and the less tangible and more subjective part of him. A further advance was made when the Orphics and Plato and other thinkers like them did away with the semi-material double and substituted the conception of the purely spiritual soul. This, I say, was a gain over the muddled conceptions that preceded it; but, like many reforms, it brought with it difficulties almost as great as those which it sought to abolish. Plato's stress upon the difference between soul and body was so extreme as to place the former in the realm of ideas or purely logical essences, while the body stayed below in the "unreal" world of space, time, and matter. So "ideal" a treatment of mind obviously put it beyond the reach of any naturalistic investigation and made impossible any explanation of particular mental events.

The great naturalists of antiquity, Democritus and Aristotle, saw the weakness of such a complete separation of mind and body, and sought in different ways once more to join together what Plato had put asunder. Democritus' method was in effect a proposal to return to the pre-Platonic identification of the psychical with the physical; on the basis of this principle he worked out an elaborate hypothesis of perception by means of material images, sent off from material objects, which, entering the sense organs, set in motion material soul atoms. Similarly, thought was to be interpreted as the less violent motion of the soul atoms set up by the much finer images from the more complex structure and relations of things. The aim of this hypoth-

esis was laudable—to formulate the indubi-
tably close relation of mind and body which
had been neglected in the Socratic-Platonic
theory. But the proposed method of formulation and explanation was too crude to stand.
Before Plato it may have been possible to
neglect the contrast between the mental and
the physical, but, once the distinction had
been pointed out, only a very unempirical
Naturalism could fail to take account of it.
The Democritean theory, moreover, had the
further disadvantage that when taken seriously it made all knowledge impossible, in-
cluding the knowledge of the Democritean
theory. It was, therefore, pretty generally
discarded as being obviously crude, and a
more critical naturalistic theory of mind was
sought in its place.

Aristotle undertook to furnish the desideratum by the hypothesis (differing essentially
from those of both Plato and Democritus) that
the soul is the form of the organism. This
suggestion had the merit of recognizing the
close relation of soul and body, which Plato
had neglected, yet avoiding the crude identification of the two in the manner of Democritus. The soul *is* not material; it is the form
of the living thing, but not the form of the
body in the sense of being its shape. It is,

rather, its essential nature and, as a thing is
what it does, the soul is the life or function-
ing of the living body. A mass of matter that
is not alive—that has no vital activity—is not
a body! And a soul which is not the vital
activity of a body is not a soul—it is nothing
at all.

This way of interpreting the soul has great
attractions and for centuries had a large following. Careful consideration of it, however,
shows that, while it applies admirably to the
situation if "soul" be taken to mean *life*, it
runs into difficulties when "soul" is taken to
mean *mind*. For Aristotle, unlike Democritus,
never lost the Platonic insight that consciousness is a very different thing from unconscious matter; the attempt to identify *soul*
with both life and mind, and therefore (implicitly) to identify the two with each other,
made his theory essentially unstable.

No substitute was suggested for it, however, until the days of the great founder of
modern Naturalism, Descartes. What I have
referred to as the essential instability of the
Aristotelian view he clearly saw and boldly
proclaimed. Going back of Aristotle to Plato,
he pointed out the essential distinction between the thinker and his body and made
fundamental to his philosophy what Professor

Whitehead has called the "bifurcation of Nature." It may be worth our while to consider one or two things about this bifurcation. The first is that its sharp contrast between the thinker and the physical world is not something new with Descartes. It goes back at least to Plato, Socrates, and the Orphics in Greece, and in India to the Upanishads. Instead of enlarging the chasm between the two, Descartes in fact diminished it; for Plato had located thinker and physical object in different worlds—one in the realm of essence or eternal nature, the other in the changing realm of existence. Descartes puts them both where they obviously belong, in the existent world of space and time and particularity. But this existent realm is exactly what we mean today by Nature; and by dividing the existent into the two mutually exclusive parts—*res extensiva* and *res cogitans*—Descartes did make clear that "bifurcation" to which Whitehead refers. The bifurcation was not new but it was now placed within nature.

The motive for this radical modification of the Aristotelian treatment of mind is obvious. It was due to the fundamental naturalistic demand for the empirical method. The true naturalist, like all systematic thinkers, likes to reduce two categories to one when he can; but, while he enjoys being monistic, he *must* be empirical. No one loved unification and rationalistic system more than Descartes. It was for this that he identified matter with space, so that the whole science of the physical world could be ultimately reduced to geometry. It was for this that he went to the extent of denying consciousness to the animals. The rationalistic naturalist within him would, doubtless, have liked also to deny consciousness to the human race, himself included. Doubtless consciousness is in the way; its presence irritates the neat mind of the rationalistic naturalist whose loyalty is first of all to system, and who frames his system independently of the disorderly and somewhat dirty facts. But though rationalism was strong in Descartes, it was balanced by a great honesty; and he knew that the one thing he could not deny was the reality of consciousness. Hence the "bifurcation of Nature," the rock upon which a large part of modern philosophy is built and against which the gates of many a new-fangled and ephemeral school have not as yet prevailed.

It is quite comprehensible that Descartes' sharp differentiation between body and mind should have postponed for many a long year any serious attempt to treat the psychical scientifically. Pseudo-attempts were indeed made in the pre-Kantian days, resulting in what was known as "Rational Psychology," and (a little later) "Faculty Psychology." The first of these was really a philosophical discussion of various problems about the soul; while the second tended to explain all the doings of the mind by reference to mental "faculties" for doing just those things—an achievement which will remind certain wicked critics of Molière's physician who explained the fact that opium puts one to sleep by learnedly referring to opium's *dormitive power*. It was largely in protest against these pseudo-naturalistic treatments of mind that the first really scientific modern school of psychology, known as Associationism, was started. The founders of the school (Hartley and several other British followers of John Locke, in the eighteenth century) were dissatisfied with rationalistic methods, and insisted that a truly naturalistic study of the mind could not be *a priori* but must start with particular and verifiable facts, and must then proceed to discover order and to formulate laws. This was a great step in advance. It was recognized that psychology should study not the self or soul but the mental states which introspection revealed. Not unnaturally the physical science of the day was taken as the model by the new psychology; and as physics and chemistry had reduced matter to molecules and atoms and then proceeded to discover the relations between atoms and the regular sequences of physical events, so associationists sought to analyze the facts of human experience revealed by introspection into their ultimate elements, and to discover the relations and laws that hold among them. These (more or less hypothetical) ultimate elements were known as ideas; they were conceived as sensory particles. Each, it was said, is characterized by its sensory quale and its temporal locus. They follow each other in ascertainable orders, the formulations of which are known as the "Laws of Association." Analysis of mental content and these laws of general sequence thus furnish the complete explanation of all the facts of mental life, and psychology becomes a kind of psychical geometry and mechanics. The mind is a collection of mental atoms which bump against each other, so to speak, and follow each other in predictable fashion. In it there can be nothing new save new sensations and these, of course, are rare after childhood. What seems to the adult to be new is not really so, but is merely a new combination of preëxisting elements. The perception of relations between things or between ideas is to be described and explained by just the togetherness of the mental elements, that is to say, consciousness of relation is just another "idea" and is ultimately sensuous. For there is, of course, no perceiver or activity. Experiences or mental elements come along one after another like freight cars in a moving train, none of them doing anything, none of them active, all just lumbering along, with no observer on hand to see them. What we take to be the experience of succession *is* just the succession of experiences; what we call the consciousness of activity or effort or concentration of attention is just a series of purely passive sensations. Emotion and will, or course, are nothing more.

Associationist psychology is a beautiful system. It was carefully thought out and artistically constructed by three generations of ingenious scholars. It is a thoroughly self-consistent and luminous description. Unfortunately, it does not describe anything that is real. Pity there should be nothing in the existent world, in the actual human mind, to correspond to it; but that is the sad truth. It is a kind of Utopia, a psychologist's dream, illumined by a light that never was on land or sea. The construction of it was a fine piece of work, but as a description of the human mind it is unrecognizable. The "ideas" out of which it builds its world are empirically undiscoverable; and the laws devised to explain the combinations and sequences of its "ideas" are altogether incapable of explaining the empirical facts of actual experience. As James so well pointed out, a succession of experiences is *not* an experience of succession. And as Aristotle pointed out long before him, we not only see and hear, we also perceive *that* we see and *that* we hear. We not only have sensations; we compare our sensations with each other. Neither of these processes can be explained or described as merely a succession of "ideas." In short, only a very small portion of the mental life can be analyzed into anything like the sensory atoms with which Associationism alone deals, or can be described and explained by the "Laws of Association." Most of the significant characters of the mind are simply omitted by this school. And its fundamental principles are so out of harmony with the major conceptions which have dominated psychology since the rise of Darwinism that as a school it is nearly dead.

I have given considerable time to Associationism because, as an episode in the progress of investigation, it is typical of much of the advance of Naturalism. It made a real contribution in setting up a new ideal for scientific psychology; but this once accomplished, its dogmatic insistence upon artificial and *a priori* categories and its neglect of the truly empirical method carried it out of the main stream into a kind of back-current, so that the steady advance of Naturalism has left it stranded and stationary on the shore.

We have not the time in this lecture to deal with the half-dozen or more schools of psychology which have followed Associationism, some of which are still with us, while others now sleep with their fathers. Each one of them has added something to our insight, each has carried farther the advance of Naturalism, but not one of them can be accepted as entirely satisfactory. No serious student of psychology can consider the present status of his science without a certain amount of discontent. Except in pathology we really do not know much more about the mind than we did forty years ago, and it is a serious question whether psychology can ever become a science in the sense in which physics and chemistry are sciences. My own opinion is

that it never can, and that there is a very
fundamental reason for this, a reason to be
found in the nature of the self as such; but
that is a question which we need not here
discuss. Aside from that, the contemporary
schools of psychological investigation show
certain weaknesses, most of which can be reduced to one or the other of the two following:
either they are mere piece-meal collections of
separate facts, or, going to the opposite extreme, they are so committed to particular
and somewhat *a priori* theories as to be blind
to facts of a kind not wanted. Those which
fall a prey to this latter weakness are dis-
loyal to the fundamental empirical method
of Naturalism. More than one really great
psychologist, and many a psychologist of
smaller caliber, has notably reduced the value
of his work by refusing to consider problems
of an essentially empirical nature because the
subject matter was (to use Münsterberg's
phrase) "*grundsätzlich ausgeschlossen.*"

This dogmatic and hence self-defeating attitude of many schools of psychology comes
to the front particularly in connection with
theories of the relation of mind and body.
And indeed, whatever self-denying ordinance
the scientist *qua* scientist may succeed in im-
posing upon himself, no naturalistic philos-

opher can avoid the necessity of giving long
and serious consideration to the mind-body
problem. It is central as no other problem is
to our concept of ourselves and of reality;
and the conclusions we come to in regard to
it, however faltering and tentative they be,
will momentarily or permanently affect the
determination of our opinion within many a
distant field. The problem is one of such radical significance that it cannot be avoided in
this lecture.

The problem is sufficiently difficult, as the
long controversy over it painfully indicates.
It has one hopeful aspect, however; namely,
the pretty obvious fact that the number of
possible solutions is narrowly limited. Since
it is plain that by "body" and "mind" we
do not mean the same thing, we are bound
to recognize that there must be some relation
between the two, and, in so far as this relation is conceived in terms of influence, there
are only four theoretical possibilities of a
general sort,* each principle sort having, of
course, its possible subdivisions. While, then,

* One of these four, moreover, is never taken seriously
—namely, the conceivable view that, though body is real
and quite distinct from mind, it exerts no causal influence either upon mind or upon its own processes; all of
the causal influence is from the mind. This view is
plainly not a form of Idealism.

we may never be able to come to a final and
demonstrable conclusion upon our question,
we can at least see what the possible answers
are and the nature of the considerations to
be adduced in proof of and against each of
these answers.

The earliest answer given to the question,
when first mind and body were distinguished
from each other, was probably this: that there
are situations, such as that in sensuous perception, in which the body influences the
mind, and other situations, such as that in
voluntary and deliberate action, in which the
mind influences the body. This was plainly
the position of Socrates and Plato. It probably was the position of Aristotle also, although his conception of the psyche as the
"form" of the organism makes his opinion
on the question at issue a little ambiguous.
The problem at length came out in perfect
clarity in the hands of Descartes, as a result
of his sharp "bifurcation of Nature." Mind
and body being now explicitly contrasted,
there was no longer any excuse for muddling
the question of their relation or the possible
answers to it. But while this is true, there
remains some uncertainty as to what Descartes' favorite answer was. I speak of a
favorite answer, for in the course of his

writings there occur at least two, possibly three, answers which he seems to adopt. One of these is that given by Mechanism or Materialism; namely, that the activities of the body are never influenced in any degree by anything mental, though the mind is certainly influenced by the body. The other answer and the one which Descartes evidently favored more and more as his thought matured, was that of Interaction. The third answer, which he may not really have intended, was that of Occasionalism. It is interesting and, I think, instructive to note the reasons or motives which attracted the mind of Descartes to each of the first two theories.

It was to the rationalistic side of Descartes' mind that Mechanism had its great attraction. One of his principal aims as a philosopher was to vindicate the essentially mathematical nature of the physical world, to exhibit it as one unitary deductive system. But the human body is a part of this system. If the necessary and rationalistic nature of the physical world is to be carried through, one must conceive all human acts as completely determined by physical laws, and never in any way influenced by the non-spatial *res cogitans*. Plainly if one starts with this rationalistic conception of the physical world, there can be no place for Interaction, and the most complete Mechanism must result. Whatever one may think of the truth of such a world-view, it is worth our while to note that the method by which it is reached is completely out of harmony with the fundamentally empirical character of Naturalism as outlined in our first lecture. And not only because of its rationalism is Mechanism inconsistent with Naturalism; it is committed also to one of the modes of thought which, in the first lecture, we envisaged as essentially anti-naturalistic—namely, the "Will-to-Believe." For if we ask how Descartes and those like him reach their rationalistic view of the physical world, it should be evident that it is not through any necessity of thought nor any balance of evidence, but solely because they like that kind of picture of the world. In short, they start with their conclusion, which they choose because of its aesthetic and emotional appeal and, having started with it in the beginning, they have no difficulty in finding it in the end.

Far different were the motives that led Descartes to his more mature belief in Interaction. To admit the influence of mind on body would, he knew, badly spoil his beautiful monistic picture of the physical world;

yet in passage after passage he asserts this
very influence; and for the obvious reason
that he plainly found it and that he was an
honest man. It was to Descartes the empiricist that Interaction made its appeal. And
whether we ourselves agree with Interaction
or with Mechanism, we must, I think, recognize that in the struggle between them in
Descartes' mind it was from Naturalism, in
the true sense, that the Interaction theory
drew its strength, while Mechanism got its
backing from thoroughly unempirical motives
—motives which in this respect were, therefore, anti-naturalistic.

There can be little doubt that a rationalistic desire for a strictly deductive universe
was the determining motive, once more, for
the beginnings of modern Materialism with
Thomas Hobbes and the French mechanists.
For Hobbes as for Descartes, the ideal for
science and for philosophy is to be found in
mathematics. The world with all its processes
is to be conceived as a kind of moving geometry. This he is sure can easily be done if we
will agree that the only cause of any kind
of change is motion. Since this conception is
the necessary condition of a completely deductive world system, it must be true. It must
be true, hence it is true; and since it is true,

the world is a completely deductive system.
Q.E.D.

But Hobbes was not altogether certain—
and never made up his mind—just how the
position of the psychical in this mechanistic
world should be stated. Plainly there were two
mutually incompatible paths to choose between; and Hobbes chose both. For one might
say that mental phenomena *are* nothing but
body—to use modern expressions, nothing
but nerve centers or nerve processes—or one
might admit the reality of mental phenomena
and their essential difference from bodily
phenomena, but insist that the mental is always caused by the physical and is never
itself a cause of anything, not even of further
mental events. A moment's reflection will, I
think, convince one that the first of these expressions of the materialistic doctrine is as
extreme a form of nonsense as the ingenuity
of the human mind can possibly concoct. To
be told in all seriousness that a man's love for
his child *is* a pinkish greyish collection of
matter in his cerebral cortex, that the north
pole *is* a logarithm, that the experience of
belief in God *is* a spiral motion among certain brain cells—to be solemnly assured of
things like these produces in a normally sane
mind a kind of dizziness seldom known even

in a mad-house. And if in one's bewilderment
one be asked how the identifications suggested
can be refuted, one will suffer the added
humiliation of being unable to say anything
at all! There is no possible refutation, no
reductio ad absurdum, of that which is already the extreme of absurdity. With a man
who proclaims it, there is nothing one can do
—nothing but leave him to the uncovenanted
mercies of a Creator who moves in a mysterious way His wonders to perform. I realize
that one sub-type of this meaningless doctrine has sought to dignify itself by adopting the name Philosophical or Watsonian
Behaviorism; but from the strong language
I have used I have nothing to retract. Nor do
I think that the Identity theory of Hobbes
has gained in strength by identifying consciousness with bodily behavior. The question
can hardly be argued. When a physical object looking like a human being makes noises
that sound like an assertion that he (or it)
is really only an unconscious talking
machine, somewhat improved over the ordinary victrola, I do not waste my time denying the assertion.

The other type of Materialism has a much
more respectable position—the hypothesis,
namely, that while both the mental and the

physical are perfectly real, and each is what
we find it to be, the physical (that is to
say, probably the cerebral cortex and its
processes) is the cause of all mental events,
whereas mental events are never the cause of
anything. Consciousness, in short, is an epi-
phenomenon, accompanying the series of
brain events, as its shadow accompanies a
moving train, but never in any way influencing either the brain events themselves or any
subsequent thoughts or feelings. This "epi-
phenomenalist" form of Materialism has been
discussed *pro* and *contra* ever since Hobbes'
time and never more thoughtfully than in the
last few years, so that there is really nothing
new to say about it. It seems unlikely that
any important new facts will be discovered or
new considerations brought to light that will
materially affect the question; so all we have
to do is just to make up our minds! This each
one must do for himself, according to what
seems to him the relative importance of the
considerations brought forward by the two
sides. These may be briefly rehearsed.

The enormous amount of evidence for the
influence of bodily upon mental states is, of
course, no argument for Materialism, since
this influence is one of the things also asserted by the theory of Interaction. Only

the parallelists deny it, and they in fact really
assert it in "*ein Bischen anderen Worten.*"
The real arguments of Epiphenomenalism
against Interaction seem to be the two following: (1) If you think out the implications
of Interaction to the end, you will find that
it can hardly be made a comprehensive system
without involving the acceptance of a real
continuing, substantial self. It is, of course,
easy to say that separate thoughts and will-
acts affect bodily conditions and activities;
but the mere stream of consciousness made up
of those separate elements is so broken, so
piece-meal, so lacking in substantivity that, if
the doctrine of Interaction is to be carried
through, consciousness must be taken as
merely the expression or behavior of some
more substantial and continuing entity which
coöperates with the brain in producing the
particular conscious states. Now such a self
would be, as Cohen puts it, "inherently in-
describable and beyond our common knowledge." "We do not, in fact, know any
unembodied self or soul, and we cannot tell
what would be its essence or inner life apart
from the consciousness of body such as gives
color, warmth, depth, and reality to our own
consciousness. And since we cannot formulate

its nature, it cannot serve as a verifiable hypothesis to explain any actual event." *

(2) The second argument of Materialism is closely related to the first—is, in fact, in a sense, merely a different expression of the same fundamental thought. To allow any slightest influence of consciousness as such upon the activities of the body would mean the surrender of the assumption (to use Cohen's excellent wording once more) that "bodily conditions and processes form a continuous series in accordance with chemico-physical laws, such as that of the conservation of energy. The introduction of purely mental or non-physical terms into the series would destroy its homogeneity and would be inconsistent with the aim and method of physiology as a natural science." †

The defender of Interaction will, I fear, have to admit both these allegations. Something may, perhaps, be said in favor of a theory which should make the stream of consciousness, with no real self involved, interact with the body and its processes; but personally I believe that the materialist is right in doubting the ultimate tenability of such a

* *Reason and Nature,* p. 301.
† *Idem.,* p. 324.

view. Most probably the interactionist will simply reply that, if all the relevant facts and considerations should finally point to the reality of a self, or should indicate that physiology is not as completely homogeneous as many physiologists hope, we should just have to make the best of it. It would, of course, be too bad to disappoint the physiologists and to do anything "inconsistent with the aim and method of physiology as a natural science." But the interactionist will suggest that the aim of finding out the truth, and the method of a genuinely empirical Naturalism, are even more important matters. And as for the conservation of energy, that is a long story. For one thing, a number of clear thinkers, such as Stumpf and Broad, are convinced that Interaction is perfectly consistent with this physical theory; and even if the interactionist does not take that view, he may successfully challenge the materialist to prove the universality of the conservation principle. It could, I think, be shown without difficulty that nothing of either an *a priori* or an empirical nature can be said in support of the view that in organic and conscious bodies the "law" of conservation holds. It is perfectly conceivable and self-consistent to suppose that in those organisms which differ from all the rest of the physical world in being conscious, this enormous exception to the usual run of things should be accompanied with the much less striking exception of a variation in the appearance and disappearance of energy.

It is worth pointing out, moreover, that, whatever we may think of the conservation of energy as an argument against Interaction, the advocate of Epiphenomenalism, at any rate, is precluded from making use of it. For the universal application of this "law" is plainly as inconsistent with Epiphenomenalism as it is with Interaction. Moreover, there is exactly the same kind of evidence in favor of the causal influence of the mental on the physical as there is for the influence of the physical on the mental. Why, then, reject one and accept the other? Or will it be said that while there is invariable and regular sequence of certain bodily activities upon certain mental activities, we should not call this a *causal* influence because "such causality remains different in type from the kind we use in physiology"? * And, if so, will not the same objection hold to ascribing causal influence to body when it influences mind? And if we are consistent and carefully refrain from using the word *cause* except as within

* Cohen, *op. cit.*, p. 324.

processes that are entirely physical, shall we really feel better by modifying our verbal expressions and saying that mental and bodily processes never *cause* each other but continuously *influence* each other? Perhaps we shall. But whether we do or not, let us realize that in saying this we have given up Materialism and accepted Interaction.

The considerations we have been discussing that point toward Interaction are of a rather negative and defensive character. There are arguments of a more positive sort—all of which, no doubt, are quite familiar to this audience. The central point of it all is the fact that the denial of Interaction involves the denial of any efficiency to consciousness. There are several different ways in which the force of this denial may be brought home to us, these different applications of the one central thought often figuring as separate arguments. Thus the very denial in itself, when one stops to think of it, is so astounding as to settle the matter for many people. In truth it would be difficult to devise an assertion not in itself meaningless or self-contradictory, that should be more utterly incredible than this. That neither perception, thought, love, hate, attention, volition has ever had any influence on any human action,

and that all men at all times would have acted
precisely as they have acted had all of them
been mere unconscious automata is something
that most of us will find very difficult to consider seriously. And exactly this is involved in
the denial of Interaction. The question cannot be avoided: do consciousness, thought,
emotion, volition have any influence upon
human behavior? There are two possible
answers to this question. One of them is
Yes, the other is *No*. Whoever ventures to say
Yes commits himself to Interaction.

The implications of the denial of Interaction are varied; several of them have often
been stressed. More than one writer has
pointed out that the development of intelligence and other mental functions, if it be
not attributed to direct divine creation, must
probably be explained through the Darwinian principle of Natural Selection. It is thus
that Darwin and his followers and evolutionary psychology in general have regularly
accounted for the mental development of
animals and men. But such an explanation
assumes as its necessary presupposition the
efficiency of consciousness.

Another way of presenting the consequences of depriving the mental of all influence consists in pointing out that unless

thoughts have some effect upon subsequent thoughts, in some manner help to determine our opinions and judgments, there can be no such thing as logical necessity, nor even probability. If the conclusion to the familiar syllogism concerning Socrates' life-prospect be determined wholly by purely physical causes and in no manner influenced by the considerations that he is a man and that all men are mortal, then there is no more proof, no more logical necessity involved than there is in the fall of the avalanche. It is, of course, thinkable that seeming logical necessity is an illusion, and that no conclusion is demonstrable or even possible. But if this be so it must apply with its full force to the conclusions drawn by Materialism. The materialistic doctrine cannot be made consistent with its own probability. If it is logically demonstrable it is certainly false.

Materialism in both the forms I have presented would appear to be an essentially crude doctrine. It will not stand before criticism. We can hardly feel surprise at the fact that toward the close of the nineteenth century it was being pretty generally discarded. But many of the philosophers and psychologists who were abandoning it did not like to go back to Interaction. The great reason for this reluctance was, of course, the very comprehensible one that Interaction allowed a non-physical, non-mechanical influence to break in upon the regular working of the laws of physics and chemistry and thus upset what otherwise would be a delightfully regular and monistic system. This argument was, of course, a direct appeal to the Will-to-Believe; so other arguments were devised. One of them was the familiar oft-quoted inconsistency between Interaction and the principle of the conservation of energy. Another was the difficulty in seeing how two things so unlike each other as the mental and the physical could interact. This second difficulty seemed stronger before the times of Hume and Kant than it does today; for we no longer feel sure that we can understand *how* two things that are *like* each other can interact; and the newer concept of causation outlined in a preceding lecture is perfectly applicable to the action and reaction and interaction of all kinds of things. However that may be, neither of the two arguments against Interaction here cited was available for Materialism. But there was a third theory of the mind-body relation which could use these arguments—a theory that went back to the great Spinoza. And it was not surprising that many a psychologist and philosopher at the close of the nineteenth century, despairing of Materialism, yet unwilling to accept Interaction, should have rushed with enthusiasm for this way out between Scylla and Charybdis. This hypothesis, as you all know, was Parallelism.

This new doctrine was most inviting. It promised everything that anyone could ask. It would render unto Caesar the things that were Caesar's, and unto God the things that were God's. In fact it would go even farther than that. It would render unto each of them, and at the same time, absolutely everything. It alone offered a way out of the two difficulties recently mentioned—that arising from the conservation of energy, and the difficulty about causal influence between unlike things. For the doctrine held that mind and body never influence each other but invariably run parallel to each other.

Thus Parallelism was a consummation devoutly to be wished, settling all our questions to the satisfaction of everyone—provided you were not so curious, or so ill mannered, as to ask how it happens that the stream of mental events and the stream of physical events run invariably so parallel. However, answers were devised to this question—not one but several. One was that mind and body were two aspects of a Tertium Quid, whose nature was entirely unknown except in this: that it was neither mental nor physical. If you did not feel satisfied with this explanation of the well-known by the utterly unimaginable, you might try this: that the mental and physical were the *appearances* of a Tertium Quid. If this seemed to you only a little worse than the preceding, you were referred to Idealistic Parallelism. This doctrine took for granted Berkeley's dictum, "*Esse est percipi*," and also the panpsychic interpretation of the physical world. Each piece of matter, on its inner side, or rather in its own reality, is a psychic center or stream, its physical character being the sensuous effects which it makes (apparently through telepathy) upon other psychic centers. To this add one more hypothesis and the problem of mind and body is solved: the psychic center of which my cerebral cortex is the appearance (in other minds) *is* my personal consciousness. This explains why my mental processes and the processes of my cortex are always parallel; for the cortical processes are nothing but the appearances (really the merely potential and non-actual appearances) of my personal consciousness.

This is a very artistic as well as a very subtle and complex hypothesis. One must admire the ingenuity displayed in its construction. Pity that the designers of it should have formulated it (inadvertently, I suspect) in such a form that its truth could be actually tested. For, of course, there is one situation in which, if the theory be correct, the cortex should completely dissolve and fail to appear—namely, when the personal consciousness (of which it is the appearance) ceases, or breaks its connection with the body, as it does at death. We open up the skull of the dead man and there—to the astonishment, I suppose, of the idealistic parallelist—we find the cortex still appearing!

My presentation of Parallelism and of its difficulties is almost unpardonably sketchy; but not, I trust, *entirely* unpardonably. For you as well as I are interested in eventually getting to the end of this lecture; and moreover, this doctrine which was so popular forty years ago is in our days being rapidly abandoned.

The three theories we have discussed, Interaction, Materialism, and Parallelism, with their variations and sub-divisions, between them exhaust the suggested solutions of the mind-body problem. I hasten to add, however, that there are several thinkers and schools of thought which, in recent years, have sought some method of avoiding the problem altogether. It is not surprising that such an attempt should have been made; for both Parallelism and Materialism offer extremely great difficulties, and, as we saw in the first lecture, there is in the philosophical mind a natural hankering after a monistic solution to every problem. There can be little doubt that this urge toward monism—and in the case of the majority of those who seek to avoid the problem, an urge toward mechanistic views—has been the chief motive in prompting these attempts to show that there really is no mind-body problem at all. Among the leaders of this enterprise may be mentioned several objective idealists, neo-realists, objective relativists, and logical positivists, such as Mr. Smuts, Dr. Carrel, Professor Lloyd Morgan, Professor Woodbridge, Professor Dewey, Professor Stout, Professor Hönigswold, Professor Reininger, Dr. Robert Blanché, Dr. Ruyer, Professor Koffka, Mr. Adrian Coates. Plainly there is no time toward the close of this lecture to deal with the various methods for avoiding a difficult problem suggested by the individuals and schools in this impressive list. At this late hour the best I can do is to state quite baldly that in my opinion all these methods and attempts, when critically considered, turn out to be utter failures, for reasons which I have elsewhere carefully stated; * and furthermore, that in most cases the failure has been due to a complete misunderstanding of what the mind-body problem really is. For instead of discussing the relation between mind events or selves, on the one hand, and bodily events on the other, most of the writers and schools mentioned above have directed their remarks to some epistemological question, such as the general relation of mind to the physical world, or the possibility of meaning and knowledge. The mind-body problem, we should remember, is as compatible with Idealism as with Realism. The only dualism it involves is the recognition that, in some sense or other, mind events and the brain events which are somehow correlated with them are not identical, yet are related.

The renewed interest which is being shown in both Europe and America in the mind-body problem is pretty fair evidence that the attempts to prove the non-existence of the problem have not been successful. A similar conclusion results from an examination of the papers on the subject presented at the recent

* See *Matter and Spirit,* Lecture III, and *Personal Realism,* Chap. XVI.

International Congress of Philosophy in Paris (August, 1937). Of the nine philosophers who there dealt directly with the mind-body problem, eight defended some type or other of Interaction; and of these eight, seven insisted upon the reality and activity of a self. I might add that a similar consensus of opinion in favor of some form of Interaction was manifest in the recent joint meeting of the American Philosophical Association (Eastern Division) and the American Catholic Philosophical Association.

It would, I think, be safe to say that there is a decided tendency today—at any rate among naturalistic thinkers—to recognize, on the one hand, that the mind-body problem is very real, very important, and not of a kind to be avoided by any epistemological or other device; and, on the other hand, to disregard and leave on one side the various solutions proposed by Parallelism. These two tendencies combined leave the issue much more clearly marked, and the hope for some sort of at least tentative decision much brighter. The Materialism of today, it should be said at once, does not share the crudities bequeathed to the school by Hobbes, Helvetius, and Holbach. It is a much more self-critical doctrine, and it seeks to avoid the absurdi-

ties of both of the older schools of Materialism. Among its leaders may be named: Durr
and Paul Cohen in Germany, Alexander,
Bertrand Russell (i.e., one of the Bertrand
Russells), and possibly Dawes Hicks in Eng-
land, Drake, Santayana, Strong, Warren,
and Sellars in this country. If one may speak
of a general trend among most of these
thinkers, it is away from an explicit Epiphenomenalism toward an attempt to modify
it by combining with it something of that
form of Materialism which taught an identity
between the mental and the physical. Thus
Durr, while distinguishing between psychical
and physical phenomena, conceives of *"Geist"*
as the ultimate entity of which psychical
phenomena are the superficial changes, while
"Materie" is taken to be the corresponding
substantial, but unknown, element under-
neath physical changes. So much understood,
Durr's final hypothesis is the identity of
Geist with *Materie*—a kind of identity-part-
nership in which *Materie* apparently has the
decisive vote. The most promising formulation of what we might call the "New
Materialism" is in my opinion that of Professor Sellars or that of Professor Swabey (if
the latter is to be classed among the material-

ists at all). For Professor Sellars, consciousness is one of the inner qualities of the brain. It is not, to be sure, a quality that one observes from without, but one that is felt from within. It is the "qualitative dimension of a brain event. It is the patterned brain event as sentient. It is because of its status that we, as conscious, participate in the being of brain events. Here and here alone are we, as conscious beings, on the inside of reality." *

Professor Sellars has put the materialist conception more persuasively than I had supposed possible. That I am not really persuaded by it is due to several considerations. One is that, as indicated by Professor Sellars' own wording, it is impossible even to express this position without, explicitly or implicitly, referring to and presupposing ourselves "as conscious beings"—for Materialism the most dangerous admission conceivable. Another of my difficulties with Professor Sellars' proposal is that I seem to be constitutionally incapable of putting real meaning into the assertion that thought, or conscious activity, *is* a quality of material objects on all fours with its primary or

* *The Philosophy of Physical Realism,* p. 414.

secondary characters.* Professor Swabey's "double-knowledge theory," as presented in his recent and most excellent work, *Being and Being Known,* would be open to the same

---

* Since this lecture was delivered Professor Sellars has given a further expression of his position in an article which is a marvel of clear exposition in a field of great difficulty and subtlety (*An Analytic Approach To The Mind-Body Problem;* Philosophical Review, XLVII, 461-487). Says Professor Sellars: "The organism is to include logically what can be known about it from the outside, what can be known about it by self-knowledge, and it is so to be thought, and consciousness is so to be thought, that consciousness can be located literally in the brain-mind." "In his own consciousness each of us is on the inside of his own brain and his consciousness is a factor intrinsic to cortical processes." Consciousness is "not a physical system but a qualitative dimension of the existential content of a highly involved physical system." It is "a feature of the content of being of cerebral activities," and is known by direct awareness, while the brain is known only indirectly and by representation, as is the case with all physical objects. Consciousness is not "an alien force interfering with the chain of causation as conceived in terms of descriptive facts." On this question "all forms of behaviorism are correct."

Greatly as I admire this remarkable piece of exposition, I am still unconvinced. I still find it very difficult to understand what can be meant by the assertion that consciousness is a feature or quality of a physical process. Possibly by further effort I may come to understand it. But while, possibly, consciousness as a stream of psychic events might be conceived in this fashion, it is immensely more difficult to accept Professor Sellars' position when one has to face the facts of knowledge and thought. Here, unless my epistemology is utterly mistaken, an active subject is necessarily implied. As Professor Sellars says: "We may try to grasp the notion

criticism if it were not for the fact that he has so far modified Professor Sellars' view as to give up its essentially materialistic character. In fact, Professor Swabey's hypothesis seems to be Interaction with the additional assertion that (in some entirely inconceivable fashion) brain and brain processes are identical with the admittedly very different conscious processes. But though I cannot agree with either of these recent re-formulations of Materialism, I must again express my admiration for their ingenuity. And, what is more important, I must point out that both of them (whether consistently or not) recognize the efficiency of consciousness and the causal influence of purpose.

Aside from specific objections to particular theories, I should add, in more general fashion, that (in my opinion, at least) this

of consciousness while recognizing that" etc. It is *we* who do the grasping and recognizing. To assert that a subject of knowledge, which grasps, recognizes, thinks, is "a feature of the content of being of cerebral activities" does not seem to make any sense at all. I should add that in his recent article Professor Sellars does not even attempt to answer the logical difficulty involved in his (necessary) acceptance of the materialist and behaviorist position concerning the inefficacy of consciousness. Where no necessity save of the physical sort is acknowledged, and the influence of logical considerations is thus denied, no claim can be made for the logical necessity, or even the logical probability, of one's own position.

whole recent movement, known sometimes as the New Materialism, has done really very little to avoid the difficulties of the Old Materialism. It would seem that the efficiency of consciousness must be either admitted or denied. If denied, all the old difficulties come back. If admitted, the New Materialism becomes something very like Interaction. Furthermore, if we enquire what new arguments are to be found for the New Materialism, none are forthcoming. The one decisive consideration for the New Materialism as for the Old is the fact that many a scientist feels reluctant to admit the causal efficiency of consciousness. Thus we come back again, as so often before, to wishful thinking.

Next to the rapid loss of Parallelism in the estimation of those dealing with the mind-body problem, perhaps the most notable tendency in the last thirty or forty years has been the steady gain of Interaction. To make a proper list of the leaders in this advance would take more time than I should give, so I shall content myself with mentioning Bergson, Driesch, Busse, Becher, Hofler, Wenzel, McDougall, Lovejoy, Whitehead (part of the time), Montague, Sheldon, Brightman, Flewelling, and the other "personalists," Hocking, Adams, Robinson, Leighton, and many

other idealists. Like Materialism, Interaction
has also gained in clarity of thought and of
expression—particularly through the careful
expositions of Busse and McDougall. Body
and mind are no longer depicted after the
manner of a twig and a bird perched upon it,
nor as two tennis players taking turns in hit-
ting a ball. The two are conceived as much
more intimately and organically related; and,
instead of alternating in the role of cause and
in the role of effect, each is seen to be constantly co-cause and co-effect. Interactionists
are divided on the question of the self. But a
large proportion of them agree with most
materialists that some sort of substantive self
is required if there is to be genuine interaction between the physical and the psychical.

I am aware that there are many naturalistic thinkers who will insist that whoever ac-
cepts the reality of a self, or believes in
Interaction or in the efficacy of purpose or in
a dualism of process, is a renegade or a foe
to Naturalism. This, of course, is the reverse
of the position I have tried to establish
throughout these lectures. Naturalism as I
have sought to present it is not to be equated
with Mechanism. It need not insist that
mechanical causation is the only kind of
causal influence. It can with perfect con-

sistency recognize a dualism of process, or a multiplicity of process, within Nature. It believes, indeed, in an orderly Nature, in a Nature of law rather than of caprice, in a Nature which shall be self-explanatory, affected not from without but from within, following not foreign legislation but its own laws. But these naturalistic beliefs are by no means incompatible with a recognition that there may well be different kinds of order and of law, and that centers of thought and volition which we know as selves may bud out, so to speak, from the tree of life, and play a genuine part in the give and take of Nature. If Naturalism be incompatible with the reality of such selves, some of us empirical thinkers who have been very sympathetic with its aims and methods will be forced, reluctantly, to enroll ourselves no longer among its friends but among its foes.

Nor am I willing to stop with this purely defensive attitude. I am minded to go further and insist that those who would magisterially read out of the naturalist camp all those who do not accept the mechanist presuppositions are themselves betraying the essential aims and the fundamental principles of Naturalism. I can, of course, understand the motive that prompts them. It is the laudable desire to promote the scientific knowledge of Nature, and so far it is worthy of praise. But in their absorption in the application of methods that have been found useful, they have often turned means into ends, and, forgetting that the attainment of truth is their great aim, they have made their tools into idols and worshipped them. Doubtless it has been useful to see how far the mechanistic interpretation of life and mind can go, but the value of this method cannot atone for blindness to the facts. As Whitehead puts it:

The man with a method good for purposes of his dominant interests is a pathological case in respect to his wider judgment on the co-ordination of this method with a more complete experience. Priests and scientists, statesmen and men in business, philosophers and mathematicians, are all alike in this respect. We all start by being empiricists. But our empiricism is confined within our immediate interests. The more clearly we grasp the intellectual analysis of a way of regulating procedure for the sake of those interests, the more decidedly we reject inclusion of evidence that refuses to be immediately harmonized with the method before us. Some of the major disasters of mankind have been produced by the narrowness of men with a good methodology.

The particular doctrine in question is that in the transformations of matter and energy which constitute the activities of an animal body, no principles can be discerned other than those which govern the activities of inorganic matter. ... The point to which I wish to draw attention is the mass of evidence lying outside the physiological method that is simply ignored in the prevalent scientific doctrine. The conduct of human affairs is entirely dominated by our recognition of foresight determining purpose and purpose issuing in conduct. Almost every sentence we utter and every judgment we form presupposes our unfailing experience of this element in life. This evidence is so overwhelming, the belief so unquestioning, the evidence of language so decisive, that it is difficult to know where to begin in demonstrating it. ... It is no solution of the problem to ignore this evidence because other operations have been explained in terms of physical and chemical laws. The existence of the problem is (by these mechanist methodologists) not even acknowledged. It is vehemently denied. Many a scientist has patiently designed experiments for the *purpose* of substantiating his belief that animal operations are motivated by no purposes. ... Scientists animated by the purpose of proving that they are purposeless constitute an interesting subject for study.*

* *The Function of Reason,* pp. 8, 9, 12.

To this magnificent passage from White-head, I need add nothing. Surely he is right in insisting that the question whether purpose ever acts causally is one to be settled by the facts and by rational considerations as they shall arise. When the defenders of some particular theory demand the acceptance of their views, not on the ground of evidence or of clear thinking, but from considerations of "methodology," or because they start (and wish the rest of us to start) with their favorite conclusion, they deserve no more attention than does any other kind of dogmatist. They have written themselves down not as real students of Nature but as followers of the *High A priori,* or zealous devotees of the Will-to-Believe, who walk by faith not by sight. They have given up the method and have been untrue to the aim of genuine Naturalism.

It may be said that in speaking thus on the part of Naturalism, I am assuming far too much authority for myself. And, indeed, I have no authority, no right to speak for Naturalism at all—I who have often publically assailed one of the schools of thought that bear its name. But while I cannot speak as a representative of Naturalism I can and must at least say this: that Naturalism must choose between accepting the aim and method which in our first lecture I attributed to it, or else frankly admit that it is not the sort of liberal, empirical, truth-seeking school that I have sought to expound and defend. We are here at the parting of the ways and we must come to a clear understanding of ourselves and of each other. We empirical thinkers have tried to go along with Naturalism, and we shall be glad to continue to do so. We have done our best to present it in a favorable light and to defend it against its defamers. But if, by the insistence of a great majority of its leaders, Naturalism identifies itself not with a desire to know the truth and to get at the truth by an unprejudiced study of the facts, but with a particular theory, formulated in advance of the facts, adhered to in defiance of the facts, and defended not because it is true but for its own sole sake, then we must definitely part company with it.

I do not anticipate any such sad parting. There is, indeed, a crude Naturalism, a dogmatic Naturalism, with which it will be impossible for us empirical thinkers to coöperate. But there is, and I believe there always will be, an empirical Naturalism whose one devotion is to the discovery of the truth about Nature.

This lecture has concerned itself with the

naturalistic study of man. The outcome of it, and of the previous lecture, has been briefly two-fold. It has shown, first, that man is not a stranger or a misfit in Nature but that he is at home in this world. He has grown out of Mother Nature as her own child. But secondly, it has become increasingly clear that this Mother Nature, with which he is at home and from which he sprang, is not a mere collection of atoms acting solely according to mechanical laws, but a much richer organic whole within which many more influences and processes and qualities of being are at work than are dreamed of in the mechanistic philosophy. When we have put life and mind into Nature, the concept of Nature is significantly enlarged. Between man and his Mother there is a certain family resemblance. It does, indeed, characterize him to realize that he has sprung from Nature; but this fact characterizes her as well.

And, to make this thought more pointed, let us at the end of this lecture come back to the question that I raised at the close of the previous lecture, namely this: Is purpose ever causally efficacious? To this question all interactionists and a number even of the materialists will answer, *Yes*. In fact, any other answer really makes nonsense of human life and human history. The thesis cannot, indeed, be proved in the way of a mathematical theorem, but I should be glad to wager that there are very few persons in this room this afternoon, very few persons anywhere in the world, who do not believe that in human conduct purpose is a *vera causa*.

Let us keep this fact in mind and with it the further fact that, according to Naturalism, there is a very real continuity and family likeness between man and his Mother Nature. He is bone of her bone, flesh of her flesh. He characterizes her as much as she characterizes him. With these two thoughts in mind it is hard to turn one's back upon the obvious suggestion that in the great organic whole, which Nature is, purpose also is at work; that in the Cosmos as a whole, as well as in our little lives, purpose is at least one of the dominating influences. It is, at any rate, perfectly consistent with a very real Naturalism to take into serious consideration the hypothesis that the Cosmos as a whole is permeated with immanent purpose, that it is a teleological and, therefore, a spiritual organism.

CHAPTER IV

NATURALISM, MORALITY, AND RELIGION

NATURALISM would be a sadly incomplete philosophy had it nothing to say upon the great question of the moral life. And, as everyone knows, upon this theme naturalists have had much to say. Here as elsewhere they have begun with criticism of the schools of thought which they found in possession of the field, and have gone on to a more positive attempt to build up an ethical principle which should be consistent with the naturalistic view of reality, and, still more important, a principle which should achieve the naturalistic aim and should be the logical outcome of the naturalistic methods. In other words, the naturalistic moralist is interested not in some abstract realm of ideal essences, but in the warm and throbbing life of human beings. It is not ideals in the abstract that he wishes to know about, but the ideal way, the best way, for men to live in this concrete world of ours. And the methods which he means to use in this quest are those that he has tried and learned to trust in his more theoretical investigations—clear and logical thinking and the use of the relevant facts.

It is plain that, having such aims and such methods, the naturalistic moralist cannot be satisfied with any form of authoritarian ethics. What the great religions have had to say about the good life may be true enough, but before their commands can be taken as binding they must show their credentials. Mere assertions of authority cannot be accepted; and if the authoritarian consents to argue the matter, he thereby gives up his appeal to authority, and puts himself on the level of reason and evidence where the naturalist will be glad to coöperate with him in their common search.

Conventional, traditional, intuitional ethics are no more trustworthy, in the opinion of the naturalist, than authoritarian. In most cases one intuition can be balanced by an opposing one: and when intuitions disagree who shall decide? The appeal to universality in moral opinion is quite useless. It is in vain that Bishop Butler says: "Let any plain honest man, before he engages in any course of action, ask himself; Is this I am going about right, or is it wrong? Is it good or is it evil? I do not in the least doubt but that these questions would be answered agreeably to truth and virtue, by almost any fair man in almost any circumstance." *

It would certainly be very convenient if all questions of morality could be settled in this simple and easy fashion, but since Butler wrote his sermons, new facts about moral convictions have come to light which show his belief in the universality of moral approval and disapproval to have been quite mistaken. Indeed, none of these new facts are really necessary: the example of St. Paul, not unknown in Butler's time, should have been sufficient to show his confidence in the agreement between all honest men unjustified. Butler and his school must therefore either appeal from rival intuitions to the common judgment seat of Reason and the Facts, or else try to avoid this surrender of the intuitional position by the hypothesis that the divergences between consciences are due to the deceptive and corrupting influences of social opinion upon an original "Simon-pure" conscience which is the same in all men. But the naturalist will want to know where such a Simon-pure conscience is to be found: and the answer—the only possible answer—will be very plain and very devastating. Such a conscience—one, that is, which never has been

* *Fifteen Sermons,* Sermon III.

subject to the misleading influences of social opinions—is to be found only in the cradle, only in the infant during those blessed days of early innocence before he has any conscience at all.

The formalistic ethics of the Kantian school will appeal to the naturalist hardly more than intuitionism. Possibly a little more. For Kant explicitly founds his doctrine upon reason. But Kant's equally explicit ruling out from ethics everything of empirical origin makes it impossible for the naturalist to go very far with him. In fact, not only in method do the two types of thinkers disagree but, seemingly, in aim as well. For the aim of the naturalistic moralist is to find a criterion for conduct, an ideal that shall be a guide for actual human living, which formalistic ethics in the nature of the case can never give. The Categorical Imperative bids us in all cases to act in such a way that the principle at the base of our conduct could be a universal law for all actors. But any principle could be a universal law if expressed with a little care. I should have no difficulty in wording even the most evil "maxim" in such fashion that it could be carried out by all men in just my place. Kant's ethics very properly stresses the universal element in morality. If a form of conduct is to be defended rationally, plainly it must be unprejudiced, it must not make the actor an exception, it must hold for all individuals in the same situation. But this gives no positive guidance as to what a man should do; nor does it offer any method or principle of choice between different possible courses of conduct each of which could be "universalized" in Kant's sense. In effect Kant tells me that I ought to do that which any and every rational being in my place ought to do. Which is doubtless true. What any and every rational being in my place ought to do, however, Kant neglects to indicate; nor is there anything in his formalistic system which will throw any light upon this question. But this question is, for the naturalist, the very center of ethics. That one ought to act in a universal way is only another form of saying that one's acts should be rationally justifiable: but the important question for us, if our ethics is to give us any guidance whatever in actual living or actual judging, is the question what kinds of acts *are* rationally justifiable. And no ethical theory which is purely formalistic and quite unempirical can give us any help in answering it.

When Naturalism faces the problem of formulating its own positive ethical doctrine, we shall find it, as in the more theoretical spheres, making several tentative hypotheses, applying its general methods in what could be almost called experimental fashion to the new material and the new problem. Among the earliest of the naturalistic proposals in the field of ethics was that suggested by David Hume—to the effect, namely, that as good empiricists we should merely observe and write down the various forms of approval and disapproval which different social groups have exemplified, and having done this much in careful and (if possible) in exhaustive fashion, we should stop there. On this view ethics ceases to be a normative science and becomes purely descriptive. The task of the moralist, thus understood, is to investigate and describe the various folk-ways, approved and disapproved customs, ways of feeling toward different types of conduct, concerning which history, anthropology, ethnology, and psychology can inform us: and to write out our results in some such way as Westermarck and others have done. Back of these various approvals and disapprovals, Hume and Westermarck and their followers assure us, we cannot go. We are not justified in judging one form of approval better than any other. If an act be approved by a given social group, then for that group and for its members that act is good: for its being approved is all that can be meant by calling it good. Morality thus becomes a wholly relative matter. Nothing is everywhere or always good: its goodness depends wholly on the opinion that certain groups entertain concerning it. The asserted universality and absoluteness of moral "laws" are thus seen to be illusory.

Though this Humean view of morality is still extremely popular in many quarters, the thoughtful naturalist will feel suspicious of it. In the first place he will want to know rather specifically what is the social group which determines the goodness or badness of an act. Every individual belongs to a large number of social groups, groups which often disagree in their approvals. Which of them shall be legislative of his duty: by whose opinion is his act to be judged good or bad? A little thought will reveal the fact that the only group which can be successfully defended as morally legislative for any individual is the group whose emotions of approval and disapproval he shares. In other words, this "social approval" view of morality turns out to be nothing but the old intuition or conscience ethics, which Naturalism is most interested in opposing.

Moreover it seems really very queer to say that all customs are equally good provided they are approved, and to assert that we have no right to distinguish between justifiable and unjustifiable approvals. It appears never to have occurred to the upholders of this view that the most important characteristic of an act is not the fact that certain people happen to approve or to disapprove of it, but rather the fact that it has these and these foreseeable consequences. A custom which, like foot-binding, leads inevitably to intense pain and prolonged inefficiency is not made *good* in the most important sense of that word by the fact that several million Chinese approve it.

And this leads to the really decisive consideration in regard to the ethics of social approval, so far at least as the naturalist is concerned. As we saw at the beginning of this lecture, he is interested in ethics because he wants to find out, if he can, the wise way to live. The Social Approval view makes no attempt to give him guidance in his search. As a practical—i.e., a moral—matter, it is of no interest to him to be told that such and such a group approve or disapprove of a given type of conduct or way of living. The probable consequences of proposed acts will throw a great deal of light on what he wants to know. The opinions and feelings of people about it will not.

It is not surprising that a large group of naturalistic thinkers sought for a long time (a few are seeking still) to find the solution to the ethical problem by the application to the moral field of a conception that elsewhere had proved most fecund; namely, evolution. Spencer's influence in this direction was strong, and many naturalists of his generation were enthusiastic in the belief that the solution of the ethical problem was finally given in the great evolutionary formula. Reinforcements to the same movement were also brought by those Nietzschians who claimed to derive their appeal to force from the Darwinian conception of the struggle for existence and the survival of the "fittest." The empirical method of Naturalism was also appealed to as a further justification for evolutionary ethics. Let us be thoroughgoing empiricists—so the argument ran: let us not attempt to lay down the ideal for human life by evolving it out of our inner consciousness; rather let us observe the

course of Nature's greatest law, and conform
our lives to it. Let Nature set the ideal—
indeed she has already done so. The tendencies to be found in her progress, the direction
marked out by her advance, these furnish the
criteria for the lives and conduct of all her
creatures.

Like several other theories tentatively
adopted by Naturalism in its early efforts
to solve its problems, this evolutionary
formula for morality hardly stands the test
of critical examination. A more carefully
conceived and more inclusively empirical
Naturalism must reject this rather hasty first
generalization of many earnest and honest
naturalistic thinkers. The difficulty with it,
as with the preceding theory, is that it does
not exactly know what it means. It is capable
of two quite different interpretations. The
one commonly accepted by its upholders presupposes the unexpressed premise that evolutionary change is synonymous with progress.
As one looks back from the lofty position
occupied by man, evolution's latest product,
upon earlier and obviously lower stages of
life, one sees that the course actually taken
by evolution has been from lower to higher,
from smaller values to greater ones. Thus,
without thinking much about it, one naturally

comes to use evolution and progress as inter-
changeable terms. But a little reflection shows
that to assert the upward trend of living
forms from lower to higher presupposes that
we know what we mean by lower and higher.
The very conception of progress takes for
granted that we possess a criterion of relative value. In other words, before we can
intelligently assert that evolutionary change
has been progress, has been from lower to
higher, from lesser to larger values, we must
already possess that criterion of value which
evolutionary change was called upon to present us with. Instead, therefore, of evolution
dictating to us our means of judging
relative value, it actually owes whatever authority it may possess to the fact that we
already know, independently of evolution,
what we mean by the better and the worse.

I said that two interpretations of evolutionary ethics were possible. The first, we
have just seen, is based upon a confusion between evolutionary change and progress. The
identification of the two, when made explicit,
is a surrender of the central doctrine of evolutionary ethics—the thesis, namely, that one
should not judge evolution but judge ourselves wholly by it—take our criterion of
values from it. If the evolutionist, therefore,

be unwilling to give up his ethical doctrine, he must give it some other interpretation than that which would identify evolutionary change as such with progress. And I see only one interpretation which will be really consistent with his thesis. This is the assertion that relative value depends upon nothing but position in the chronological series. When it is said that we should not first make up our ideas of good and evil and judge evolution by them, but should put ourselves in line with Nature's changes whatever they may be, and help on the cosmic trend in the direction which it chooses, the meaning must be that of two stages or events in the cosmic series *that* is the better which is chronologically the later. Take, let us say, the series of conditions and events known as Roman history. The corrupt third century A.D. we must consider better than the sturdy and admirable third century B.C. because it was later. The condition of the earth a million years hence will be better than its condition today, because and only because it will be farther along in the evolutionary series. Scientists feel fairly sure that at some distant point in the future, changes in heat and moisture will be such that the earth can no longer support human life, and only the fishes, or perhaps the bugs, will survive. Such a condition, however, on the present hypothesis will be "better"—because later—than the present, and evolutionary ethics therefore calls upon us to put ourselves in line with the direction evolution is taking, and do our best to bring about that blessed consummation. I do not exaggerate the absurdity of the position. But there is no way out of it save the admission that not all change is evolution but only *progressive* change: and this admission, as we have seen, is a complete surrender of evolutionary ethics. It is not evolutionary ethics because it presupposes a criterion of good and bad not derived from evolution. The central ethical problem for Naturalism is where this criterion shall be found.

Naturalism does not assert that this is the only problem of ethics. The freedom or determination of the will in moral choice, the meaning and nature of moral responsibility, the basis of moral praise and blame for the actor as distinct from his act—these and other problems are real and have often been discussed. But for Naturalism they are either derivative or of secondary importance. As I have more than once suggested, the primary practical—i.e., moral—question for the naturalist reads: What is the wise way, the justifiable, defensible, reasonable way to live? The obvious answer to this question would seem to be: the wise act, the wise life, is the act or life that brings about the good rather than the evil. So at least thinks the naturalist. Since his interest is concentrated not upon a realm of essences or of abstract ideals, but upon this world of living men and women, of concrete, specific deeds in space and time, of pleasures, pains, achievements, failures, aims, strivings, and defeats, the object of his ethical search is the rewarding, the "worthwhile," the empirically and rationally justifiable life: the life that results in "good" rather than in "evil." Almost necessarily, almost as the logical consequence of his naturalistic aim and method, his ethical principle will be eudaemonistic or utilitarian: it will see the character of the deed and of the life in the kind of consequences which they produce.

How, then, shall "good" consequences be defined? Here is the next question. Plainly it is the much discussed question as to the nature and basis of value. Volumes have been written upon this, and presumably new volumes are at this moment being written upon it, and further volumes will be begun next year and the year after. Value theory is relatively

young among philosophical disciplines and our
time is witnessing its most rapid period of
growth. It will, therefore, be impossible in the
limited space of this lecture to go in any detail
into the merits of the question. Fortunately the
only part of the huge question which is immediately relevant to our purposes is the general
attitude toward it of most naturalistic moral-
ists. Among these there has been pretty fair
agreement in the conviction that value or
"good" is dependent upon and relative to
desire or liking. Before sentient life appeared
upon our globe there were gold and diamonds,
flowers and fruits, sunsets, breezes, rolling
thunder: but none of these things were either
good or beautiful, bad or ugly. They had
spatial and temporal characters, sizes, shapes,
positions, possibly colors, odors, sounds: but
value they did not have. None of them were
either better or worse, either more beautiful
or more ugly, than any other. We may, indeed, properly enough speak of beautiful
sunsets, delightful fruits, sweet sounds, etc.,
before the appearance of sentient life: but
this is an elliptical form of expression, and
we mean by it that the sunsets, fruits, sounds,
would have been desired, appreciated, liked,
had some form of conscious life been present
to enjoy and like them. With the appearance

of the first desiring and appreciative animal on this earth, value, or the difference between good and bad, came into being.

For Naturalism, then, value is the character possessed by an object or event in virtue of the fact that some sentient being wants it or likes it when he gets it. Anything is good to the extent to which it is desired or liked by someone, and nothing is good except in so far as it is liked or desired. Desire and liking are primary and fundamental. It is really putting the cart before the horse to say that things are desired or liked because they are good: the truth is they are good because they are liked or desired.

Upon this matter most naturalists are agreed. But when the attempt is made to apply this doctrine to psychology, as it were, and to determine specifically what things are actually good in the sense indicated, we come upon a divergence of opinion. It was not unnatural that the earliest answer of Naturalism to the problem, what things are good, should have been hedonistic. Acts are good or bad, it was agreed, in virtue of their consequences: and "good consequences" was taken to mean pleasurable consequences. The only intrinsically good consequences, in other words, were held to be the pleasurable conscious states of sentient beings.

It was in some such way that the doctrines of Hedonism were formulated. Good conduct, so this school maintains, is to be defined as conduct which produces pleasure, or (more exactly) the largest obtainable balance of pleasure over pain. The meaning of moral obligation is derived from this: one ought to act in such fashion as to bring about the largest hedonic balance. We may call this the ethical thesis of Hedonism.

In view of the theory of value recently stated—the dependence of value upon liking and desire—this ethical thesis plainly takes for granted and is based upon a psychological thesis. This psychological thesis may be stated as follows: pleasant-feeling states are the only things that are ever desired, or ever liked when obtained. Or: it is psychologically impossible for anyone ever to like or to desire anything but pleasure.

That this psychological thesis is necessary for the defense of the ethical thesis is, I think, obvious enough. A somewhat bizarre illustration may make it plainer. An enthusiastic individual rises in your town meeting, club, or Sunday service, and urges that it is the duty and the sole duty of each one of you to sing, hum, or whistle the Lost Chord into the ears of every man, woman, and child of his acquaintance. The greatest Lost Chord to the greatest number is his motto. Now before you accept his conviction as to your duty, you will want at least to be assured that every man, woman, and child wants or likes to hear the Lost Chord, and wants or likes nothing else. Unless that be the case, you will insist, you can see no reason why you ought to furnish Lost Chord music and that alone: why whistling the Lost Chord must be considered the only form of the good life. Doubtless it is well to give pleasure to one's fellows, but this is because one's fellows like pleasure: and one cannot show that only pleasure should be given them until it is first shown that pleasure is the only thing they want or like.

What I have called the ethical thesis of Hedonism, therefore, stands or falls with the psychological thesis. And in judging of this, the consistent naturalist, with his trust in science, will look to psychology and enquire of the psychologist. A hundred years ago many of the psychologists accepted the view that pleasure is, in the last analysis, the only thing that the human mind does or can like. As everyone knows, since then the situation has been completely transformed. It is doubtful whether there is today a single reputable psychologist who supports the hedonistic theory of motivation. This change has been due chiefly to a more critical analysis of the meaning of "pleasure," and to new knowledge concerning the facts of motivation. The assertion that pleasure alone is or can be desired, we now see, was largely due to a hasty identification of "pleasure" with the object of desire (so that the assertion of the possibility of wanting something besides pleasure was made a contradiction in terms), and to the related confusion of pleasure with objective satisfaction or achievement of purpose. And since the influence of Darwinism has made its way into psychology we have learned that the activity both of men and of animals is no such sophisticated and intellectual an affair as the hedonistic theory would indicate, but is initiated and guided by instincts, urges, drives. The particular form given to the "instinct theory" of motivation by James, McDougall, or any other individual psychologist may be challenged; but the substitution of present native urges and the purposes built upon them, for imagined future subjective feeling states, has become practically universal among students of motivation.

Since the psychological thesis of Hedonism is no longer tenable, the more critical naturalist has given up the ethical Hedonism that was dependent upon it. He no longer seeks to justify conduct by appeal to one very limited type of "good" consequences, or to find intrinsic value in subjective states alone. All things are good which any sentient being wants or likes: and the things which sentient beings like and want are innumerable. Pleasure is one of them, but so are material things, acts, objective situations, other peoples' feelings, social conditions, and, most important of all, the objective achievement of purposes. Most important of all, I say, because the achievement of purpose is the thing which the mature human mind cares for more than it cares for anything else.

The ethical doctrine of the more critical naturalist, therefore, comes to something like the following: good conduct is rationally justifiable conduct, and this means conduct for the sake of the greatest relevant values. These values, as I have said, may be of any sort. To act for the sake of the simple pleasures of oneself or of others is good— provided, at least, such action does not stand in the way of the achievement of larger values. The *larger* value outweighs the small

one as a justification of action. And by larger
values are meant achievements or consequences which are liked by more people, or
more intensely desired and appreciated, or
(and this is important) those that are richer
in and more productive of further values,
of further and more organic and massive
achievements of human purpose. Naturalism,
I have said, recognizes the relevance of even
the simplest and smallest values: but, it does
not fail to recognize at their immensely
greater worth the higher values of the life of
the spirit. To label this kind of utilitarian
ethics "materialistic" is merely to betray one's
ignorance. There is no intellectual development, no mystical state of the soul, no benefi-
cent economic adjustment, no victory of
peace, no union of human hearts and reconciliation of races, no achievements of faith,
no glory of unselfish love, no religious bene-
diction, which fails of its due appreciation or
of its lofty position among the discriminated
values of critical Naturalism. The good life
is the life that helps to make real these things.
To act for the sake of them is the content of
duty.

From what I have said it will be evident
that naturalistic ethics has been steadily ex-
panding, steadily advancing from a more

crude to a more critical and more inclusive
form. Those of you who have heard the three
preceding lectures will note that naturalistic
ethics in this respect has run parallel to the
developments of Naturalism in the scientific
and philosophical fields. Thus the hedonistic
view, with its narrow definition of value and
its primitive psychology of motivation, went
not badly with the equally vain conception
of a crude Naturalism which could see in life
and mind nothing more than new repetitions
of old chemical laws. Similarly, the wider
appreciation of human values and the more
critical insight into the nature of human
motives and conduct are congruous with the
larger cosmic outlook of a critical Naturalism, with its empirical recognition of selves
and of some kind of immanent teleology within
the universe. It is, I expect, true that natural
science as such can do but little in detail with
this teleological conception: cosmic purposiveness cannot explain or predict particular events. But naturalistic philosophy,
which is not so limited, and whose interest lies
not so much in particulars as in the general
nature of the Cosmos, can and must give
serious consideration to the seemingly teleological aspect of Reality and its possible
significance. The naturalistic philosopher is,

indeed, empirical in his thought, but he cannot limit his thought to a listing of discovered facts. Philosophy must speculate as well as record.

If we throw a rapid glance back over the considerations that have occupied us in these lectures, there is forced upon our inward eye, as at least a very genuine possibility, the vision of Reality as an organic whole to some extent guided by an inner and immanent purposiveness. This conception of immanent teleology has been held by many thinkers since the days of Aristotle, but not often has the question been faced what is implied by it. When one seeks to answer honestly this question of the implications of the organic view, and to accept the logical consequences of the conception involved, it becomes at once evident that one is facing a tremendously important and crucial cosmic possibility. For if immanent purpose be purpose, it cannot be divorced from mind. An utterly unconscious purpose belongs among round squares. And if one asks, further, how immanent cosmic purpose can be efficient, the only answer would seem to be that its relation to the total physical universe would, in outline, be somewhat like the relation between the human will and the human body which it inhabits. Thus one seems led on from the conception of an organic universe to the conception of an indwelling mind which expresses itself in all the activities, great and small, of the Cosmos. The concept of the universe thus suggested is plainly not unrelated to that attitude toward the Determiner of Destiny which is Religion. It may, then, be worth our while to devote the few moments left us to a brief discussion of the relation between Religion and Naturalism.

There can be no doubt that soon after their inception, and during a long portion of their historical courses, the naturalistic and the religious tendencies of the human mind and of the human race were antithetical and at times hostile. The reasons for this hostility are plain. Religion in its earlier stages stood for a kind of Supernaturalism which, could it have had its way unimpeded, would have blocked at every step the persistent attempt of Naturalism to build up a conception of cosmic order and relative comprehensibility. Naturalism, on the other hand, in its earlier stages, frequently if not invariably took into consideration only a part of the cosmic whole, and rejected as unreal whatever part of Reality could not be readily subsumed under its partial, not fully empirical, too easily for-

mulated categories. Progress in the development of Naturalism, as we have seen, has
consisted chiefly in admitting to its picture of
Reality newly discovered facts, and logical
deductions from old facts which an earlier
and hasty generalization had ruled out. The
first formulations were meagre, crude, abstract, and simple in the extreme. At first only
water or some of the popularly recognized
"elements" were admitted to the rank of the
truly real. Later on, material atoms took the
place of the "elements." But the aspects of
the real world thus arbitrarily excluded were
gradually recognized and directly or indirectly admitted. Thus the concept of "Nature" was steadily enlarged and became con-
tinually more complex. With this growth of
content and complexity Nature began to lose
its early abstract and purely mechanical
character. Instead of being the amorphous
sand-heap pictured by a crude Naturalism, it
began to take on, for the critical naturalist,
an organic character. Inherent tendencies,
and something like immanent purpose,
loomed mistily but massively before the eyes
of the student of Nature. We are now in the
midst of this process and we cannot as yet
tell where or how far it will lead us.

The development of the religious concept

of the Cosmos has been, in a sense, comple-
mentary to that of Naturalism. Beginning,
as we have seen, with a view essentially supernatural, it has tended to a steadily more and
more orderly picture of Reality. The Yahve
of primitive Israel is the almost lawless god
of the mountain and the storm. He has "un-
accountable moods." He interferes with the
somewhat orderly ways of Nature. You never
can tell what He may do. But with the rise
of the Hebrew prophets an order is per-
ceived in His seeming disorderliness. He re-
veals Himself as law-giving and law-abiding;
and as always having been such, though the
earlier generations had been blind to His
laws. Meanwhile, Zeus and the gods of Greece,
Jupiter and the gods of Rome, together with
the devas of the Rig Veda go through essentially the same development. For many centuries Christian theologians still continued
to use God to stop gaps in natural events
not otherwise explicable, but in our day this
attitude toward the Divine is rapidly disap-
pearing. More and more the God whom intelligent and deeply religious men believe in
is escaping the limits of a supernatural an-
thropomorphism: closer and closer He is coming to that Nature toward which Naturalism
also seems to be tending.

I hasten to add that by no means all the present tendencies within Religion or all those within Naturalism are in the direction of mutual toleration and sympathetic understanding. There are centrifugal as well as centripetal forces at work. Within Naturalism, as we have seen, there is still a strong school of extreme mechanists who, like the Old Guard, will die sooner than surrender, and who, if they are to die at all, will "die hard." Doubtless the appeal of the Single Formula will always intrigue and dominate certain natively monistic minds who simply will not have their neat and tidy little physical world cluttered up with such things as teleology and an efficient consciousness. Nor do I anticipate that any lasting and important movement toward religion will come out of the enthusiasm of certain physicists over panpsychism and indeterminism. Among the leaders of religious thought, moreover, there is a growing school as hostile to any reconciliation with Naturalism as are the most "hardboiled" mechanists. These reverting theologians are more numerous in Europe than in America, but even in this country they are increasing in number and influence. Though of several different schools—the more reactionary Catholics, both Roman and

Anglican, Fundamentalists, Barthians, and others—they share a common nostalgia for the days of unquestioned authority, a common suspicion of reason, and what might be called a common despair of all human thought and effort. This despair and defeatism beckon them back to a non-reasoning and passive supernaturalism and eschatology. The whole movement is thoroughly out of sympathy with the kind of immanent teleology on the basis of which alone it would be possible for liberal religious and liberal naturalistic thinkers to coöperate.

But while the centrifugal and reactionary forces in both camps are still strong, strong also—and increasingly strong—are the centripetal and unitive tendencies. Both religious thought and naturalistic thought, if one takes a long view of the whole, are becoming steadily though slowly less crude, more critical, and inclusive; less purely analytic, microscopic, and "minute," more philosophic and synoptic.

If there is to be further coöperation between religious and naturalistic liberals it must probably take its start largely from the common acceptance of the kind of teleology involved in the thought of the Cosmos as essentially organic. And before anything like

profound agreement between the two can be
reached, it will be necessary for each to think
out more clearly than many have as yet done
the implications of that fundamental concept.

Many philosophically minded naturalists,
like many objective idealists, are willing and
eager to recognize a teleological factor within
Reality, but would prefer not to be specific
as to exactly what this shall mean. But the
use of words without meaning is fatal to all
clear thinking in either philosophy or science.
And I submit that the words *teleological* and
purposeful refer to *purpose*, and that purpose necessarily involves consciousness. If it
does not, then the word does not mean anything. An unconscious purpose is what the
German language calls an *Unding:* it is a
self-contradiction. It need not mean a clearly
defined concept of a distant goal: it need not
involve elaborate "design" or the employ-
ment of a series of "means"—though at times
it well may include all this: but some degree
of conscious urge and of intelligence is the
irreducible minimum involved in the word
purpose. If the "teleological aspect" of Nature or of Reality is merely read into it by
the outside observer, if it be purely a matter
of "*als ob,*" then to assert that the processes
of Nature are purposive is simply false, and

if we are honest we shall say so. Whoever recognizes in the Cosmos a dynamic and teleological character recognizes within it a character that belongs only to mind. A Naturalism that does this is not far from Religion.

The leaders of religious thought, on the other hand, must think out with honesty and care what is involved in this fundamental belief that there is efficient purpose in the Cosmos. I take it that all those who believe that the world exhibits purpose consider that purpose efficient. The seeming teleology does not merely *happen* to be there: purpose (or the Purposer) really *does something*. The question, therefore, should be squarely faced (though, oddly enough, it has rarely been raised) *how* purpose can be efficient. Are there any places or cases in which we find purpose actually producing or influencing an event, and if so where? And if we really believe that purpose does affect anything, in what manner do we, in what manner can we, conceive it to operate? Plainly we do not find purpose operative in the movements of a machine. Everything there goes by purely mechanical forces. Nor in the making of the machine do we find anything else. Nor are we any nearer seeing the activity of efficient purpose when we watch a man making things,

or doing things, with his hands. Hands, after
all, are just physical things, and all we can
see while watching them move is a repetition
of the sort of thing we see in the movement
of a machine. Where then does purpose come
in, where do we find a case of its actually
influencing movement? When one faces this
question the answer becomes plain. The only
case we know anything about in which purpose is genuinely efficient is in our own im-
pulsive and volitional action. We find it only
in the influence of our minds upon our bodies.
If we do not find it there we find it nowhere.
We can go farther than that. Only in the act
of a mind immanent within a body can we conceive, or put meaning into, the efficiency of
purpose. Here we know well what the phrase
means, here we have the direct kind of experience that Pragmatism rightly insists is
requisite to any meaning; for we all know the
experience of purposing to move our limbs
and feeling our effort efficient and successful.
There is no experience more common than
this: in fact it is chiefly from this experience
that our whole notion of efficiency gets its
meaning. But, so far as I can see, except for
this direct influence of an immanent and purposive mind upon and within its body, there
is no way in which the assertion of the effi-

cient action of purpose upon the physical world can be made really meaningful.

The bearing of this conclusion upon the question of cosmic teleology is obvious and crucial. If purpose is efficient in the universe outside of man and animals, it would seem that it must be of the indwelling sort. We can conceive of a purely transcendent God, we can conceive of His entertaining purposes concerning the physical world, but to assert further that He carries out these purposes upon that world without being immanent within it is to say something in words to which no experimental meaning can be attached. If God acts on matter in any other than the immanent way, how shall He be conceived as doing it? Does He do it with His hands? Does God have hands? . . . Only if the divine teleology, which theology asserts, be immanent—only if God's relation to His world be in some general way like the relation of our minds to our bodies—can we really conceive in more than verbal fashion that His purpose is efficient.

It is plain that such a type of teleology is immensely more harmonious with the general position of a liberal Naturalism than the concept of a transcendent God acting from without upon a dead material world could pos-

sibly be. And once a liberal Naturalism and
a liberal Religion have accepted the concept
of an organic and teleological universe, and
have thought out, as indicated above, the
inevitable implications of such a view, it is
plain that each will have taken a long step
toward the position of the other. For a century their lines of advance have been slowly
approximating, and in our times this tendency is marked. They have not met. It is
possible they never may. It is not too much,
however, to say that they seem to be pointing toward the same goal. We cannot as yet
make out with certainty and in detail what
this goal will be, but its general outlines may
be at least vaguely guessed. Critical Naturalism seems to be finding its "Nature" in possession of more and more of the characters
men have commonly thought of as "divine,"
while the leaders of liberal religion tend increasingly to find their God in Nature—not
in the mechanical Nature of crude Naturalism, but in the enlarged and transformed concept of Reality, with *all* its characters, which
a self-consistent Naturalism is beginning to
see. Such an approximation, such a joining
of lines, such a union of forces, was foreseen
three centuries ago by the eyes of the last of
the Hebrew prophets, the "God-intoxicated"

Spinoza, in his conception of the One and inclusive Reality, which he significantly referred to as "*Deus sive Natura.*"

This union of a completed Naturalism and an enlightened Religion, if it ever comes about, will be the consummation of both; presumably the last term in a long series. But intimations of it have not been lacking at unexpected places all along the way. Even in the dark earliest stages of man's long journey strange gleams of its profound truth have suddenly streamed forth. In the Biblical account of Jehovah's first introduction to Moses and to the Children of Israel, we find a strange and striking instance of this sudden light. Moses, it will be recalled, was wandering over Mount Sinai when he came upon a sight which riveted his attention: a fire which burned without consuming its fuel. As he approached it he heard a voice saying, "Put off thy shoes from off thy feet, for the place whereon thou standest is holy ground." It was the voice of God. Moses obeyed and received the command to carry a message to his oppressed people in Egypt. And when he asked the name of the as yet unknown God, and who it was that was sending him back to His people, the voice replied: "I AM THAT

I AM. Thus shalt thou say unto the Children of Israel: I AM hath sent me."

There are two things about this magnificent reply that are worthy of attention. The name of God is "I AM." The essential thing about the Divine is its reality. God is the Real as such. When religious thought reaches its ultimate meaning, it will always find that nothing short of the totality of the Real can satisfy it, just as religious feeling will never be able to rest in anything less inclusive. About the existence of God in this high sense there can be no doubt. For His reality there is an unanswerable ontological demonstration.

The other significant thing in this reply of Jehovah is the assertion, "I am *that I am.*" God's reality is beyond doubting; but what of His nature? This is the real question about God: the question which has pursued thinking men throughout the ages and still "doth tease us out of thought." And it is to this question that the words cited are the first and great reply. "I am that I am." I am that which I shall turn out to be. Would you know the nature of the Divine? Search, and search, and again search!

The aim of the religious man and the aim of the scientist and of the naturalistic philosopher are closely related. They share a common task. This task is the progressive discovery of more and more of the truth concerning Reality. Every humble increase of scientific information, every addition to our knowledge of human psychology, every widening and deepening of our religious experience, is an increase in our knowledge of God. We are reaching a point where the thoroughly empirical naturalist and the honest and sincerely religious thinker, no longer enemies, may join forces in their common undertaking: the deeper understanding of *Deus sive Natura:* the endless and uncompletable but infinitely exhilarating and rewarding search into the nature of Him whose best definition is still to be found in the words of the Exodus Jehovah: "I AM THAT I AM."

INDEX

Anaximenes, 20–22
Animism, as a method, 18
Aristotle, 8, 22–24, 28–32, 35, 48, 57, 58, 60, 97–100, 105, 165
Associationism, 102–105
Astronomy, 34–37
Authoritarian ethics, 144

Belief in authority, 10–12
Bergson, Henri, 71, 78, 85, 86
Bifurcation of nature, the, 100, 101
Bruno, Giordano, 37, 38, 42
Burnet, John, 19
Butler, Bishop, 144, 145

Causation, 47–57
Cohen, Morris, 72, 73, 77, 78, 116, 117
Compton, Arthur, 52
Concept of Nature, 6–10
Copernicus, Nikolaus, 35
Crude and critical Naturalism, 8, 9, 32–34

Darwin, Charles, 60, 62, 70, 151
Democritus, 18, 21–24, 38, 97–99
Descartes, René, 38, 39, 41, 59, 99–101, 109–112
DeVries, Hugo, 61
Dogmatism, 12
Driesch, Hans, 66, 78

Eddington, Sir Arthur, 52

Einstein, Albert, 42, 52
Eldridge, Professor, 86
Emergent evolution, 87–93
Evolutionary ethics, 151–155
Explanation, 8, 58

Formalistic ethics, 146, 147

Galileo, 36
Genes, the, 68–71

Hedonism, 158–162
Hobbes, Thomas, 112, 113, 115
Hopkins, Mark, 87
Hume, David, 48–50, 52–54, 123, 148, 149

Instrumentalism, 4
Intuitional ethics, 144, 145, 146

James, William, 26, 105, 161

Kant, Immanuel, 49, 50, 123, 146, 147
Kepler, Johann, 36

Lamarck, Jean, 60, 63, 74–76
Leucippus, 18, 21, 23, 38
Linnaeus (Carl von Linne), 60
Loeb, Jacques, 72, 73
Lovejoy, Arthur, 36, 91

McDougall, William, 7, 89, 161

Materialism, 2, 112–114, 129–134

Mechanism, 2, 63–65, 72, 73, 83, 84, 85, 110, 111

Mendel, Johann, 62

Mill, John Stuart, 80, 81

Mind, early concepts, 96, 97

Mind and body, Epiphenomenalism, 110, 111, 114–117; Identity theory, 96, 97, 98, 113, 114; Interaction theory, 100, 101, 109, 111, 112, 117–123, 129, 134, 135; Parallelism, 123–127, 129

Naturalism, as an aim, 1–3, 4, 16, 17; as a method, 4, 5, 16, 17, 22; as a system, 16, 17

Newton, Sir Isaac, 41

Parmenides, 21, 38

Planck, Max, 52

Plato, 21, 22, 27, 48, 96–100

Pragmatism, 7

Prentice, E. Parmalee, 31

Prescott, William H., 16

Primitive man, 6

Ptolemaic system, the, 35, 36, 40

Rationalism, 13–15, 16, 38, 39, 40

Religion, 166–170, 172, 174–178

Renaissance, 1

Russell, Bertrand, 45, 54

Self, the, 116–118

Shull, Professor, 64, 70, 71, 89

Social Approval, 148–151

Socrates, 21, 25, 26, 48

Spencer, Herbert, 87, 151

Spinoza, Benedict, 123

Stebbing, Miss, 52

Supernaturalism, 5, 8, 9, 10, 12

Swabey, Professor, 56–57

Teleology, 23–26, 27–30, 40–42, 85, 141, 142, 164, 165, 171, 172, 174

Thales, 19, 20

Value, 156–158

Vitalism, 76–78, 79, 83, 84

Weismann, August, 62

Westermarck, Edward, 148

Whitehead, Alfred, 42, 137–139

Will-to-Believe, the, 3, 15, 16, 22

Wolff, Gustav, 66, 67, 81